C000023325

MONOCHROME

Black & White in Branding

GINGKO PRESS

MONOCHROME
Black & White in Branding

ISBN 978-1-58423-542-2

First Published in the United States of America by
Gingko Press by arrangement with
Sandu Publishing Co., Ltd.

Text edited by Gingko Press.

Gingko Press, Inc.
1321 Fifth Street
Berkeley, CA 94710 USA
Tel: (510) 898 1195
Fax: (510) 898 1196
Email: books@gingkopress.com
www.gingkopress.com

Copyright © 2014 by Sandu Publishing
First published in 2014 by Sandu Publishing

Sponsored by Design 360°
– Concept and Design Magazine

Edited and produced by
Sandu Publishing Co., Ltd.
Book design, concepts & art direction by
Sandu Publishing Co., Ltd.
Chief Editor: Wang Shaoqiang
sandu.publishing@gmail.com
www.sandupublishing.com

Printed and bound in China

Contents

Preface
by Jeanniffer Burnes (La Tortillería)

Monochrome depicts a collection of brands, exposing the raw sense of their personality, their strong origin, their endless possibilities and their limitless future. The collection presented in this significant project reminds us that we are responsible for developing good design, for reinventing the world – for innovating every time we give birth to a new brand that represents, more than a product or service, a lifestyle with its own unique personality.

We believe it is imperative that a brand works in black and white first, in order for its counterpart in color to achieve its purpose of bringing a brand to life. There is a certain presence and elegance that colors cannot achieve alone. Thus, the invaluable job black and white possesses emphasizes the best of every detail and thought, without cluttering the brand. As a result, they take the audience straight to the point by focusing on the brand's essence and removing other distractions. It might be true, that there is an unconscious need for the world to polarize the future and make things simpler. In a world full of choices, our decisions would be much easier if we saw them under a different light; one that only reflects brightness, where someway, somehow colors are hidden or, on the contrary, one that evolves in darkness where the absence of color leaves no confusion. Black and white brings the audience straight to the point by stripping a brand bare of unnecessary detail, letting you appreciate the detail for what it is. Even then, as Monochrome shows, there is room for shades, tonalities and shadows, which become a close family that branches out into different opportunities. A brand has to mature until it becomes a land post in our minds and stays there forever, where words are no longer required and one icon can say it all.

Creating a compilation of the best ways a brand has been represented is no easy task. A brand has to move you to achieve its purpose. Every time a brand is born it is of uttermost importance to begin from basic form. A brand is a work of art that encompasses the experience and quite often the instinct of a skillful creative director and the careful coordination of a creative team to produce it. It can take several hours, days or weeks to develop a brand and each agency has its own way of reproducing the thoughts and ideas that flood their minds and reflect the exact image of what it is meant to be.

Black and white is simple and timeless. It strips a brand to its basic form and allows the audience to appreciate its personality as we move towards its impending evolution.

Monochrome, one color, is art reduced to presence and absence. A collection that is unequivocally appropriate for this binary digital world we live in, which clearly exposes that reducing everything to 1 and 0, bright and dark, does not mean a brand is the result of a cold calculation made by a machine or a program, but the essence of the human spirit.

La Tortillería

Originally founded in an old tortilla factory, La Tortillería is a creative company with a passion for images and words, with the exceptional ability of turning them into an exquisite reflection of an idea. They create, brand, design, publish and advertise; blending creativity and functionality, giving each project a unique personality. They are creative problem solvers who begin with the finished product in mind; either starting from scratch or from an outlined plan. They make things happen come hell or high water.

Topshop Showspace AW13

Logo, signage, projections, café disposables, step and repeat backdrops and more for Topshop's Showspace during London Fashion Week AW13.

Design: Johanna Bonnevier
Photography: Johan Berglund

saad branding+design

In order to emphasize the new era the studio was entering, it was necessary to reposition its image and align it with all its differentiation points: personalized service, the innovative character of the projects and, mainly, the palpable results that branding and design combined had been providing to its clients. For the development of the studio's new image, an extensive research process took place, including: scenario, competitors, benchmarks, target audience and trends and from their analysis, all the brand's strategies were drawn. The brand was built under three main pillars: the perfect synchrony between branding and design, the creation of brands that talk to their audience in an unique and personal way and notable results. The minimal visual identity portrays a craft-like appeal, which denotes the exclusivity and customized service the studio offers. From there, a flexible and sophisticated brand was created — which is what can be expected from all of the brands under saad branding+design's signature.

Branding/Design Direction: Lucas Saad
Design: Carlos Bauer

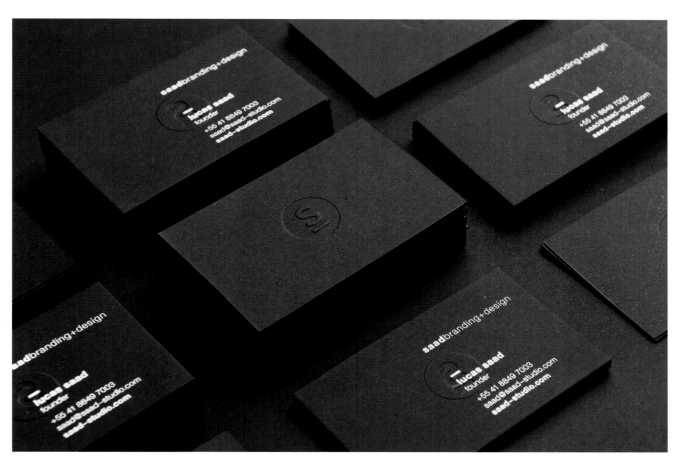

Mangoola Coal Opening Invitation

When it comes to coal mines, imagery usually springs to mind that is big, bold and blunt. But when developing an invitation for Xstrata's Mangoola Coal Mine, End of Work decided to challenge convention and create something unexpectedly subtle and delicate. The name Mangoola has indigenous Australian origins and is thought to mean 'place of the black cockatoo.' This was the image that served as inspiration for the invitation.

Intricate feather patterns laser cut into rich black card emit an air of luxury fit for such a valuable resource. The gorgeous black cockatoo flying out of the event invitation is a bit like a canary in a coal mine…

Design: End of Work

María Vogel

Maria Vogel is an up and coming fashion designer in Latin America. Anagrama's goal for this project was to develop a brand that was convincing, sober, and above all, portrayed Maria's vision — all this without competing with her imposing designs.

Based on the first geometric typefaces of modernism, they designed the typeface 'Vogel Display' in which they emphasized acute angles and modified some of the characters, providing it with a personality of its own.

Venturing into high-end markets has proven to be a bigger challenge for emerging fashion brands due to strong international competition and a more educated and demanding audience. Anagrama's work concludes in the materialization of a solid brand that shows maturity, sobriety and attitude before one of the most selective markets. It also sets itself apart as a real alternative to the top fashion houses around the world.

Design Agency: Anagrama
Design: Sebastián Padilla, Mike Herrera
Photography: Marco+Chuy

Self Promotion

"Self Promotion" showcases the selected portfolio of Yerevan Dilanchian, including various commercial branding projects along with self initiated works.

The collection assumes a signature geometric approach and explores tactility through faceted surfaces and bespoke textures and finishes.

Design: Yerevan Dilanchian

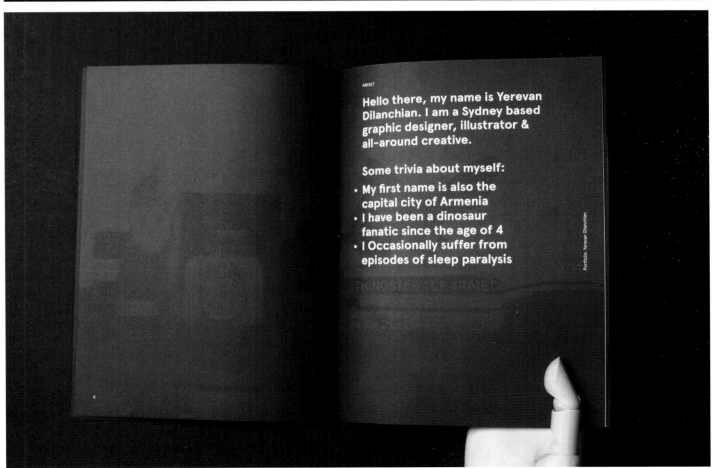

ABOUT

Hello there, my name is Yerevan Dilanchian. I am a Sydney based graphic designer, illustrator & all-around creative.

Some trivia about myself:
• My first name is also the capital city of Armenia
• I have been a dinosaur fanatic since the age of 4
• I Occasionally suffer from episodes of sleep paralysis

Portfolio: Yerevan Dilanchian

UBAR

Using clear and easily accessible imagery and colors, UBAR's branding concept achieves its aim of becoming instantly recognizable and memorable amongst the wealth of culinary competition in Philadelphia. Underlining the 'U' in the wordmark draws focus to the name while simultaneously allowing for a seamless continuation of the idea throughout, making further connections of name and place with consumers. The bold type, set against open space, ensures comfortability in a relaxed setting and encourages familiarity.

Design: Simon McWhinnie

OBR

OBR is the acronym for Open Building Research, an architecture studio based in Italy.

The main concept was expansion and the creation of new ideas, thus the letters 'OBR' have been trimmed. They now appear more open, giving a sense of broadmindedness.

Design Agency: Artiva Design
Design: Daniele De Batté, Davide Sossi
Photography: Mariela Apollonio

Blackout Tattoo Workshop

Blackout Tattoo Workshop is a new tattoo studio based in Kiev,
Ukraine. The studio is notable for its extremely high professionalism
and its gifted and skilled artists. The designer's goal was to accentuate
the exclusiveness of service, so the chosen identity had to be
radically different from other studios. Thus, all of those traditional
attributes of modern tattoo culture such as tribals, tattoo machines,
ribbons, gothic typography and so on were rejected right away. The
artists working for Blackout are rather serious guys, therefore the
designer chose an uncompromising minimalistic style. Tattooing
is a sacred act, so a mysterious tinge was added. The black circle
represents both a black dot (one stab of the tattooist's needle) and
the basis of the Universe. All begins with the dot and the origin of
everything is emptiness.

Design/Art Direction: Sasha Astron

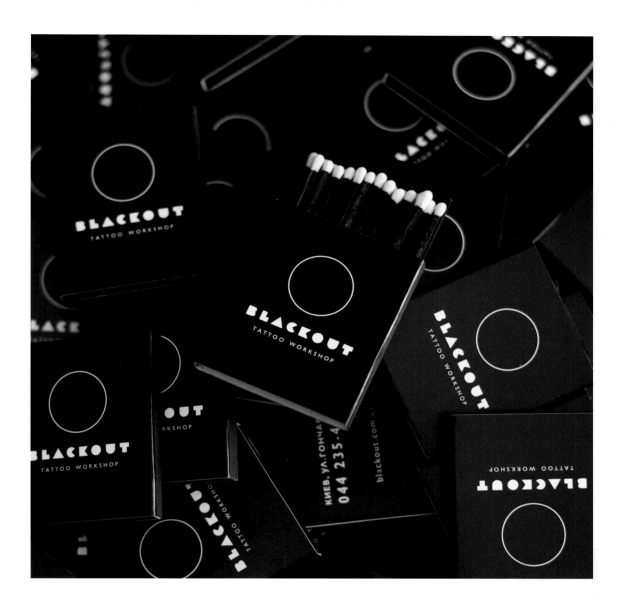

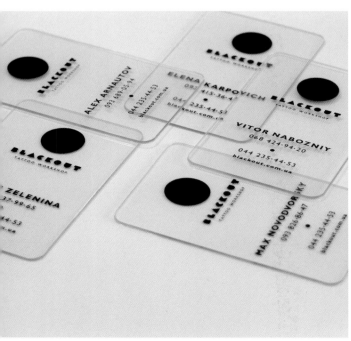

WKND

WKND is a club that proposes a great variety of quality activities. Its multifaceted and energetic nature was conveyed in the development of the logo and the graphic identity. Every element in the logo can stand on its own, so as to bring enrichment to the various formats. The promotion occured gradually and it relied heavily on images of Lugano in order to underline how WKND is the most important, historic and renowned venue of the cities' nightlife.

Design: Luciano Marx, Aris Zenone

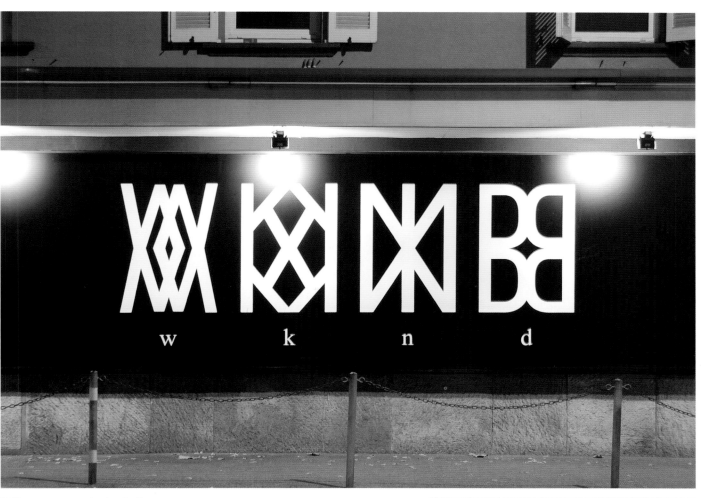

WKND
Via Trevano 56
6900 Lugano
Switzerland

AL 74

Graphic identity for the restaurant AL 74, Lugano. The choice of the typography was made in line with the choice of furniture — soft strokes and smooth corners. The wavy line emphasizes the Mediterranean cuisine.

Design: Luciano Marx

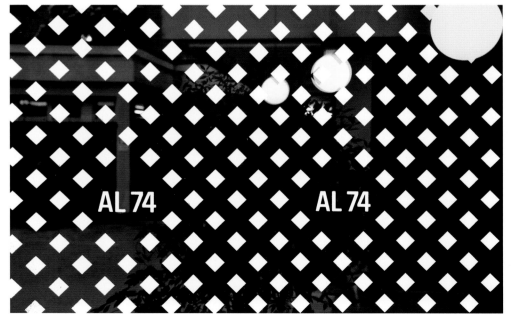

Studio Total

In mid 2010, Studio Total became Sweden and Scandinavia's best known PR agency. Since then, their advertising campaigns have attracted the attention of millions of people worldwide.

Snask was commissioned to rebrand Studio Total. The team created the brand around credibility, elegance and mystique. They conceived a visual identity where the name – Studio Total – wasn't part of the logotype, and where the icon – ST – was printed white on white. To mystify things even more, Snask created a set of Shakesperian icons that represent Studio Total's culture, values and vision.

Design Agency: Snask
Design: Jens Nilsson

House of Liza

Established in 2010, House of Liza is a boutique that sells handpicked, expertly curated pieces of vintage clothing from designers who were experimental and pioneering in previous decades. Recently, it introduced a brand new identity design by kissmiklos.

kissmiklos wanted to create a strong concept that reflected the ethos of House of Liza. His starting point is based on House of Liza's unusual, yet simple and effective display system and their vast, white shop with clean lines and a contemporary feel, where clothes are displayed on a series of lined coat hangers that hang from the ceiling. kissmiklos knew that the new visual identity had to be as elegant, fashionable and as strong as the new venue. One of the basic elements of the interior design is the coat hanger, reflecting fashion and vintage. The shape of the logo recalls the name plates of old shops and shows the place of operation.

Graphic Design: kissmiklos
Photography: Jonhaton Griggs
Interior Design: Torsten Neeland

Salon1

kissmiklos created the identity, web design, interior and exterior design and concept for this small German fashion boutique.

Design: kissmiklos
Photography: Sören Münzer, Fanni Kovács, kissmiklos

SHOWROOM &
er neue Lieblingsladen

—

EINZELSTÜCKE *von*
jungen DESIGNERN

—

ÜR FRAUEN/MÄNNER

s-a-l-o-n-1.com

Radical City

Radical City is the title of the exhibition on Italian Radical Architecture at the "Archivio di Stato"(Public Records Office) in Turin.

The graphic identity shows a modular structure; a white grid on black background that recalls the "Monumento continuo (the Continuous Monument)," a project by Superstudio.

Design Agency: Artiva Design
Design: Daniele De Batté, Davide Sossi

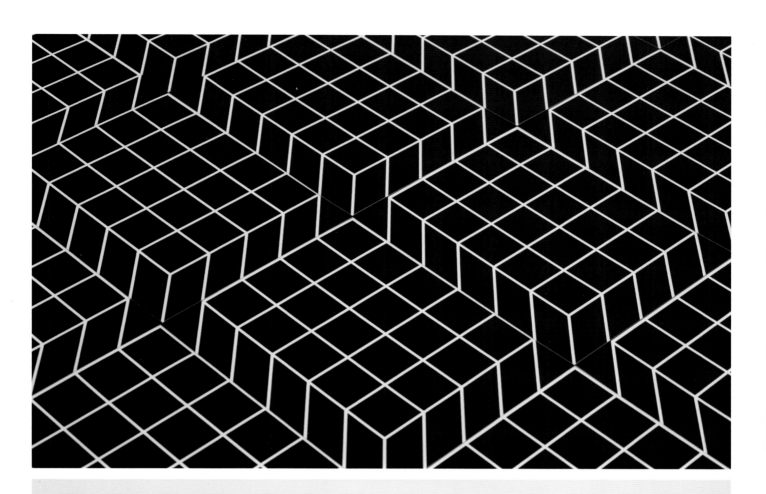

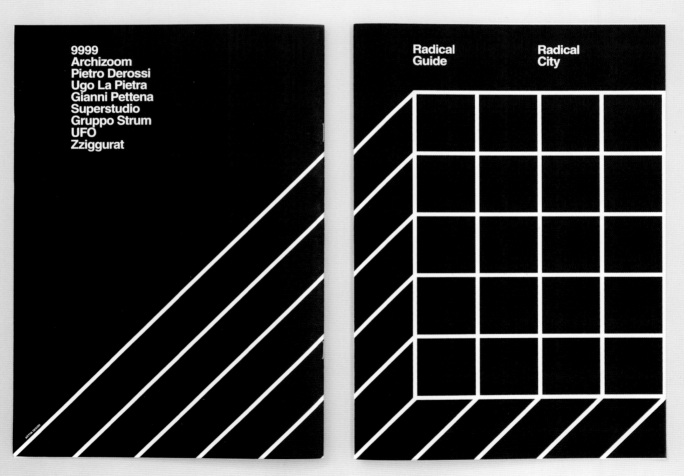

9999
Archizoom
Pietro Derossi
Ugo La Pietra
Gianni Pettena
Superstudio
Gruppo Strum
UFO
Zziggurat

Radical City

Discoteca

La discoteca è il luogo dove
i giovani possono esprimere
la loro creatività al pari dei
coetanei inglesi e americani.
È lo spazio del coinvolgimento
sensoriale: il Piper.

Mobile M+ Yau Ma Tei

Mobile M+ Yau Ma Tei is the first in a series of pre-opening 'nomadic' exhibitions curated by
M+, the new museum for visual culture in the West Kowloon Cultural District in Hong Kong.
As a multi-site exhibition of six large-scale installations in a local 'artless' area, Mobile M+ Yau Ma
Tei is thus a product of turning the supposed disadvantage of being 'rootless' into an advantage
by realizing projects that would not have been possible in a single museum building. This event
had great impact on introducing contemporary art to the public.

Design Agency: TGIF
Design Direction: Gary Tong
Design: Mandy Yuen, Ash Lam

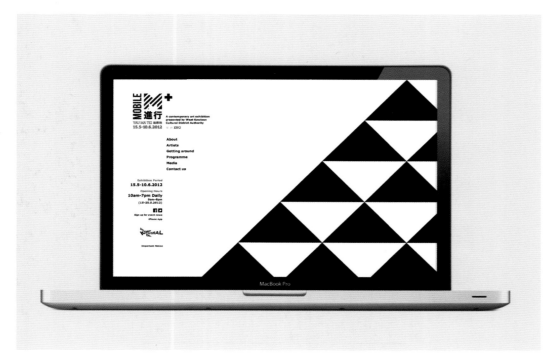

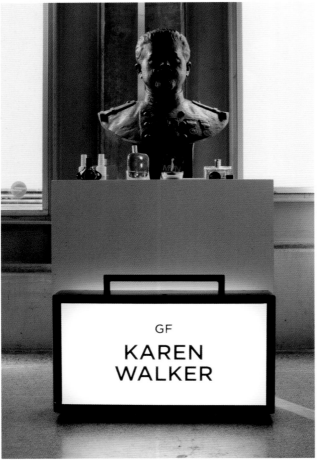

The Department Store

Branding for The Department Store, Auckland's ultimate boutique shopping experience.

Design Agency: Brogen Averill Studio
Photography: Tom Roberton

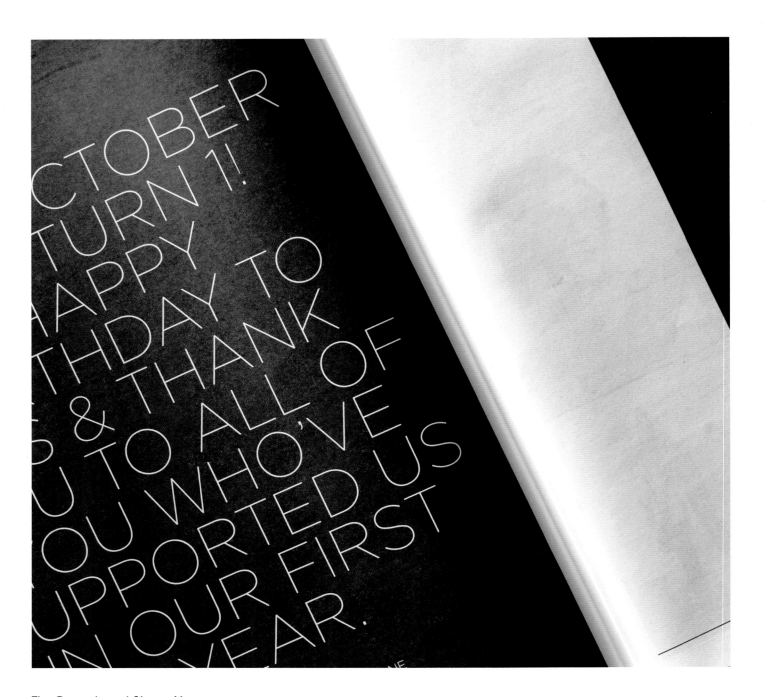

The Department Store - Newspaper

Newspaper design for The Department Store, Auckland's ultimate boutique shopping experience.

Design Agency: Brogen Averill Studio
Photography: Tom Roberton

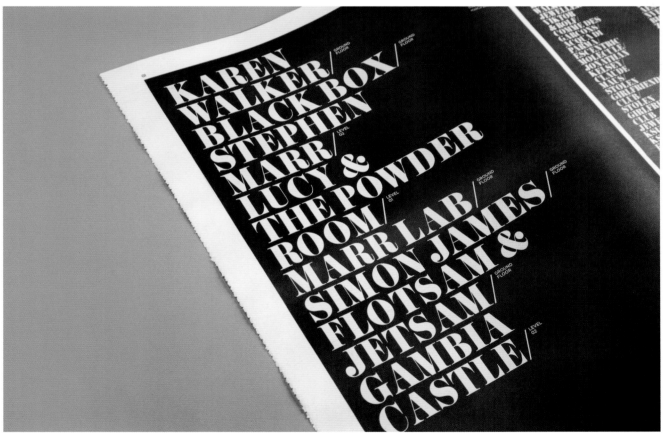

Kabiri

Kabiri is a designer jewellery store based in London and launched in June 2004 by Nathalie Kabiri. The shop continues to lead the way in contemporary designer jewellery, where each season fresh new designers are introduced as Nathalie searches the globe to curate the very best individual pieces and unique collections. Bunch was invited to rebrand their range of promotional materials. The characteristic letter K, derived from the logotype, was used as a device that gave unique personality to minimalistic packaging. In close collaboration with Wrapology, who were in charge of production, great attention to detail was applied in the selection of materials, finishes, textures and assembly so that the final outcome would feel both contemporary and luxurious.

Design Agency: Bunch
Creative Direction: Denis Kovac

Nosive Strukture

Nosive Strukture is a structural engineering studio with an unconventional attitude towards business, working environments and life itself. Equally inspired by their unique approach and their studio space, Bunch developed a stark, technical identity based on tensegrity structures and a black and white palette, which was applied to stationery, signage, website and various other applications. Which included triplexed business cards, cardboard file folders with die cuts and a direct mailer featuring a custom made, laser cut, tensegrity model.

Design Agency: Bunch
Creative Direction: Denis Kovac

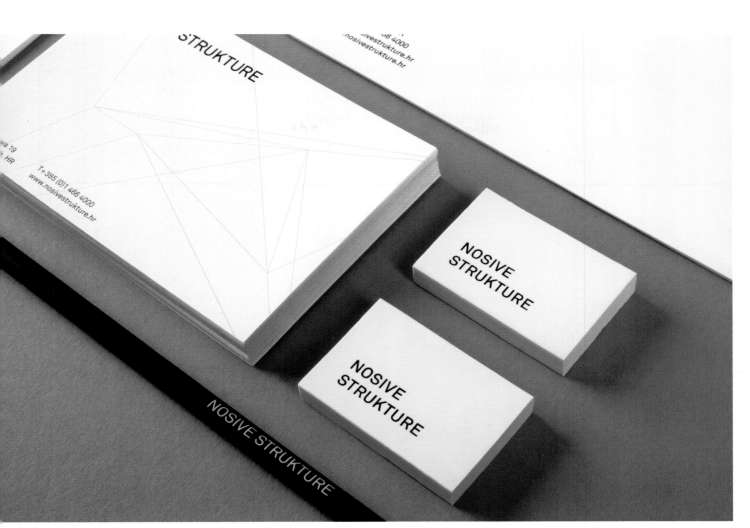

NOSIVE
STRUKTURE

NOSIVE
STRUKTURE

NOSIVE STRUKTURE

STRUKTURE

T+385 (0)1 466 4000
www.nosivestrukture.hr

Nosive strukture d.o.o.
Jurkovićeva 19
10000 Zagreb, HR

ULAZ NA
DRUGA VRATA →

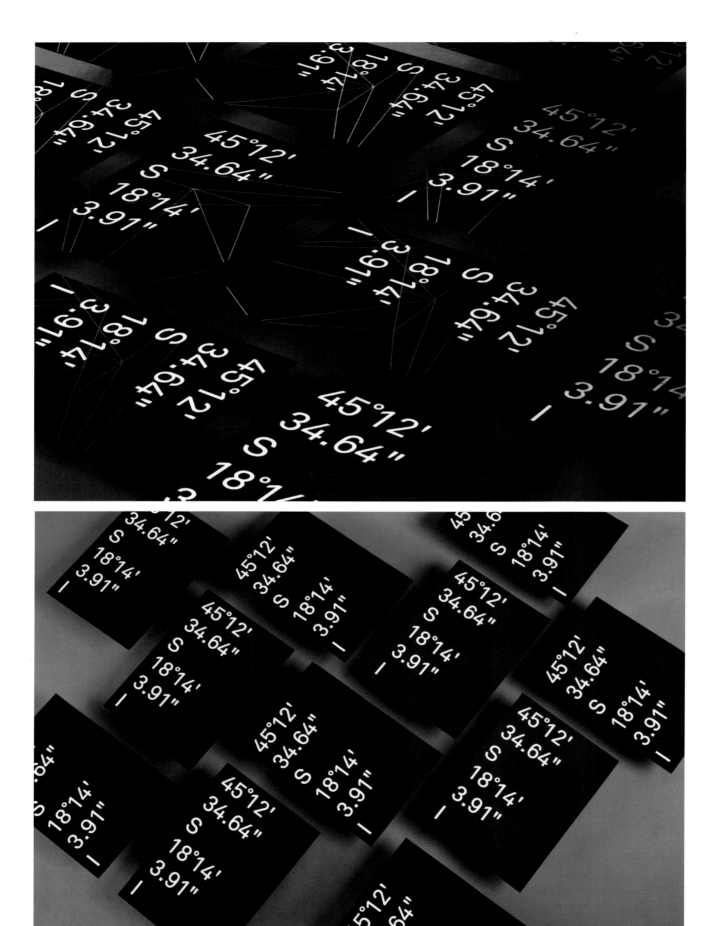

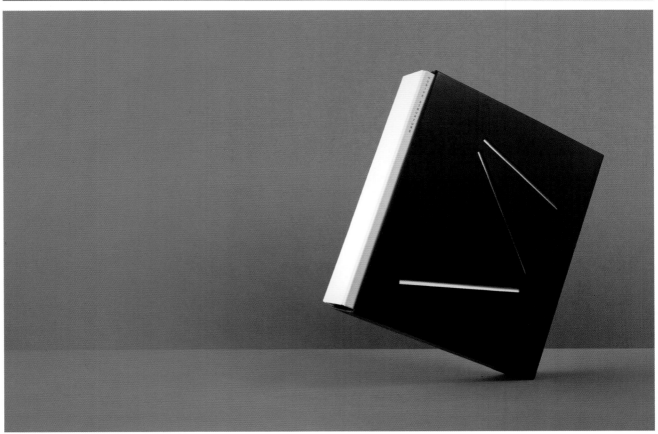

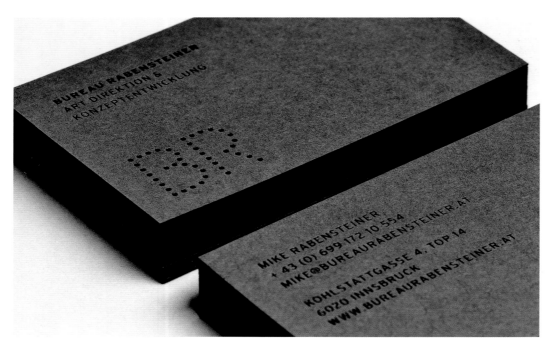

Bureau Rabensteiner

Bureau Rabensteiner stands for minimalistic and pure design. This motto is reflected in their stationery. They strove to communicate their style in a simple and discrete way. Timeless, with a touch of 'old school.' Simple, but peppered with details like wood handle rubber stamps, bookmarks and individual notebooks. They have a passion for black and white that is reflected not only in their design work but also in their studio culture and most importantly in the identity design of their Bureau. Instead of using color, they focused on high quality materials and extra finishing, like hot foil embossing.

Design Agency: Bureau Rabensteiner
Creative Direction: Mike Rabensteiner

Hyde + Hyde Architects

Hyde + Hyde are a progressive, award winning architectural practice with projects across Europe. Their work is defined by a rigorous consistency of attitude and research, rather than appealing to a particular style.

Smörgåsbord were asked to create a full identity program designed to compliment their values, vision and ambition – giving centre stage to the architecture.

Concept/Creative Direction: Smörgåsbord

Essence

Identity design for a chauffeur company in London, where tradition and innovation are seemingly contradictory. kissmiklos wanted to return to the origin of the chauffeur. Words came to his mind like old labels, name plates, cylinder, carriage and the 17th, 18th and 19th centuries. In the 19th century, the horse-drawn carriage was a fixture on the streets of London.

When kissmiklos researched the chauffeur's history, he found a drawing of King William III in a carriage and chose to incorporate this drawing into the identity.

While he was creating the identity, he moved between two worlds, the past and present. The traditional composition is reminiscent of the past, but the renewed style is clearly in the present.

Design: kissmiklos

Hotel Ambrose

Ambrose is a little hotel in Montreal. The hotel occupies two Victorian style buildings built in 1910. kissmiklos wanted to design a logotype that was a fresh take on classic Victorian style. He began by looking at Victorian letters and studying their character styles. He then drew his interpretations by hand. Once he developed the final form, he scanned the images and refined the lines and style. The font created was called Titillium. He cut the logotype from a number of places so it became more fresh and stylish. The contrast between the logotype script style and the complementary font san serif style created a nice single unit. He expanded the basis identity and created a number of other concepts, including wine labels, the 'Clean Room' card, room numbers and floor information tables.

Design: kissmiklos

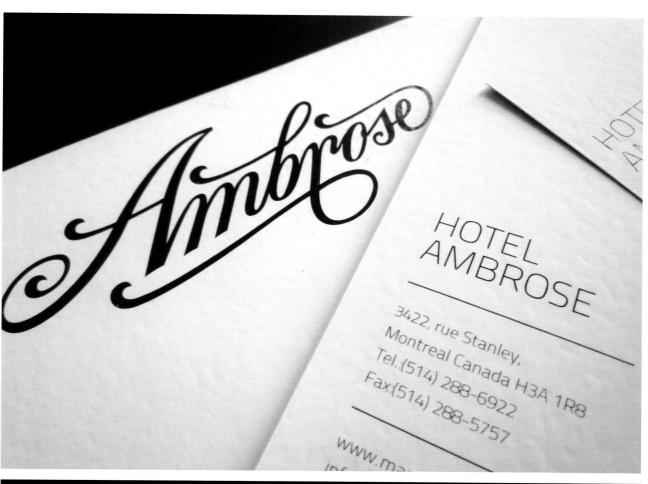

Meier Seefeld

Meier Seefeld is a women´s clothing boutique located in the mountains of Tyrol, Austria. The identity was designed to convey understated luxury in a comfortable atmosphere to both visitors and locals. The notion of traditional alpine winter sport chic is combined with a modern perspective on fashion and the zeitgeist of the village Seefeld.

Design Agency: Bureau Rabensteiner
Design: Mike Rabensteiner, Isabella Meischberger

N. Daniels Wien

This is the stationery design for N. Daniels, a rep and photo producer in Vienna. It's simple, cool and thermo sensitive. The black color of the varnish fades at body temperature — as soon as you hold it in your hands you literally produce an image created by your body. It's a dynamic and living design — the business cards are little polaroids with a constantly changing surface. All these cards might start looking similar, but with your personal 'touch,' you brand them individually.

Design Agency: Bureau Rabensteiner
Creative Direction: Mike Rabensteiner
Design: Isabella Meischberger

Ruben Hestholm

Visual identity for Ruben Hestholm, a Norwegian photographer in the Sandnes/Stavanger area. Hestholm primarily focuses on family, youth, pregnancy and children portraits. However, Hestholm wanted to enter the commercial market and his first step into that market was hiring Daniel Broksta to completely overhaul his visual identity and style in favor of a more clean and modern profile that would appeal to his new audience. The design also kept current customers in mind and didn't become too radical.

The identity is based on different cameras on different surfaces.

Design/Illustration: Daniel Broksta

Giahi

Giahi is a series of specialized tattoo and piercing studios located in Zurich, Switzerland.

The custom type designed for the logo is riddled with detail and conveys the artful and precise process of tattoo-making. The tiny, sharp peaks and crevices found in the type directly associate with the moment and accuracy of the tattooing needle piercing human skin. There is a gold-stamped droplet in the closed counter of the logo's letter 'A', a tribute to the everlasting effect of ink in human skin. The golden cross symbol at the bottom of the logotype is a salute to the brand's Swiss nationality. The logotype layout and weight is heavily influenced by the art and insignia on the leather jackets of American biker gangs of the 1960's. While the weight of the logo's typography conveys the toughness and coarseness associated with tattoos, the minute and elaborate markings and details speak of the precision and craftsmanship typical of Switzerland and its devoted clock makers.

Design Agency: Anagrama

White Ribbon Foundation

White Ribbon, Australia's campaign to stop violence against women 2011. White Ribbon is a national body in support of primary prevention programs to stop violence against women, culminating in the annual White Ribbon Day in November. Holt redesigned the identity for the organization to create a more masculine mark that would consolidate the foundation's visual language and create differentiation in a cluttered charity-day market. The introduction of a strong geometric shape for the ribbon device speaks to their target audience, while the concept of an underline rule is utilized to create emphasis. The identity can be adapted to a number of varying formats to create a unified brand.

Design Agency: Holt Design, We Think
Brand Design: Holt/Christopher Holt
Campaign: Mike Newman, Simone Bartley

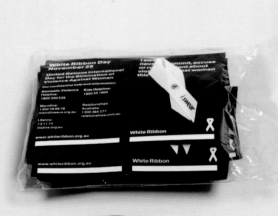

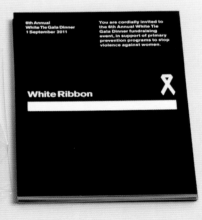

Azede Jean-Pierre F/W 2013 Lookbook

Lookbook created to promote the Azede Jean-Pierre Fall/Winter 2013 Collection. It was sent out to various stores and to press. The prints in the collection featured a line screen animation that enabled the clothing to animate on the wearer, with the animation triggered by her movement. Joseph Veazey duplicated this process in the lookbook, with the cover of the lookbook booklet and the price sheet animating as they are pulled from their sleeves.

Design: Joseph Veazey

Azede Jean-Pierre S/S 2014 Presentation Invite

Invitation created for the Azede Jean-Pierre Spring/Summer 2014 Presentation. The collection consisted of prints and forms that were inspired by beetles, insects, sea slugs and other members of the smaller majority. Various species of insects suspended in clear plastic resin blocks were used as a small gift and reminder of the show.

Design: Joseph Veazey

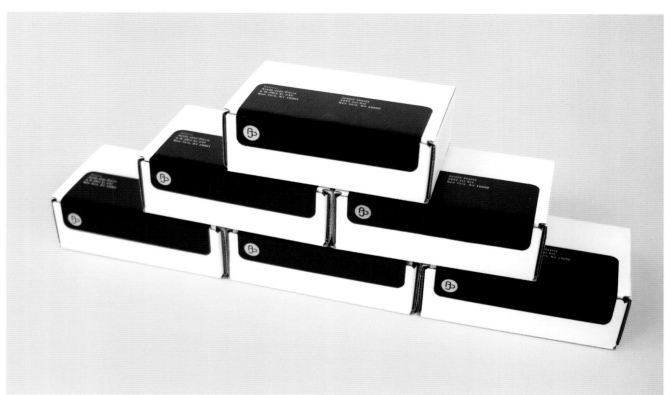

Promotion of Taller de Guionistas

The Rainy Monday made this advertising campaign for Fundación Taller de Guionistas (an academic initiative of Rodar y Rodar Productions) under the communication concept: 'You have the word.' They created and designed different pieces to promote the academic year for this school of future screenwriters.

Design: The Rainy Monday

FIRM

Folga developed the naming and identity for a barber shop named FIRM in Kiev, Ukraine. The team also developed illustration and provided practical input for its interior design.

Agency: Folga
Design: Boris Zelenkevich, Andrey Zhulidin
Illustration: Andrey Zhulidin

Frankie's Fine Foods

Identity and hospitality paraphernalia developed for Frankie's Fine Foods Restaurant, located on the outskirts of Sydney.

The print collateral assumes a black and white scheme, accompanied by hand-lettering accents, which add an organic vibe to the dining experience.

Design: Yerevan Dilanchian

Accents Decoration

In this project, La Tortillería's main goal was to highlight the meaning of an accent and its importance in different settings to create a unique space. With that in mind, they decided to give a face-lift to their image for their sixth anniversary, marking the beginning of this new phase. The ultimate makeover included a new logo, website, shopping bags, tags, stationery and presentation materials, all which are the undeniable portrait of absolute style.

Design: La Tortillería

Stories

BVD was commissioned to create a strong and totally unique café experience: from concept and name, to graphic profile and packaging. The concept needed to be warm, welcoming, honest and genuine and targeted to young professionals.

Black, white and stainless steel are blended with warm wood. The old fashioned café-feeling is expressed by things like a board with old, detachable letters and traditional cups and trays. The graphics are clean and simple, but at the same time surprising and playful. The design exudes personality, quality, style and a big city feeling.

Design: BVD

Trafiq

Identity, interior graphics, web and package design were created for Trafiq
— a club, bar and restaurant in Budapest.

Design: kissmiklos

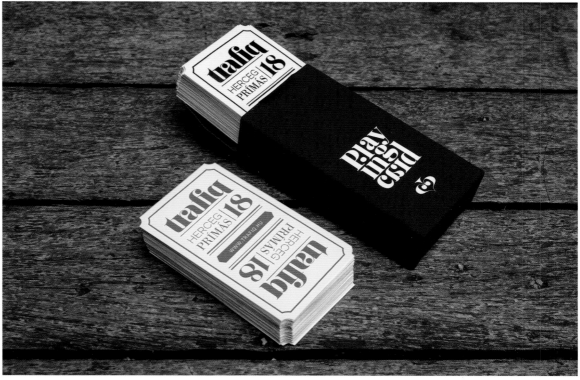

Bodega 8

Bodega Ocho is a traditional, regional Mexican cuisine restaurant and authentic bar. It required an image that emphasized its intriguing character, full of mystery, in a relaxed atmosphere. For that reason, La Tortillería's goal was to create distinctive, highly graphic black and white work, something uncomplicated but unique. The final product allowed them to use different variants of the logo, applied to different items and fabrics — from business stationery to shopping bags, fabric napkins to distinctively embossed mason jars. They developed a stylish yet fresh identity, making sure Bodega Ocho's image left an imprint on its client's minds forever.

Design Agency: La Tortillería
Creative Direction: Zita Arcq

Sweet Boutique

Sweet Boutique is a gourmet style bakery that creates exquisite treats with the finest ingredients and deliciously amazing flavors. For this project, La Tortillería created the entire brand identity of the boutique, logo, stationery, and the packaging materials.

Design Agency: La Tortillería
Creative Direction: Zita Arcq, Sonia Saldaña
Design: Karen Mata

Coffee & Kitchen

The color world, in black and white combined with brown, determines the interior design along with the corporate design of the Austrian daytime restaurant, Coffee & Kitchen. moodley brand identity has consciously avoided branding printed material, however different logo stickers convey the image of a relaxed and informal restaurant atmosphere. The casual handwriting font intensifies this feeling even more.

Design Agency: moodley brand identity
Creative Direction: Mike Fuisz
Design: Nicole Lugitsch
Photography: Marion Luttenberger

Shovel & Bell

Shovel & Bell is the latest up-market gelateria and cafe in Guangzhou, China. The brief was to create an artisanal gelato brand with an emphasis on experience, quality and taste. Shovel & Bell's vision was to use traditional preparation methods for making gelato and premium ingredients, versus industrial production and preparation. Their customers would be working adults who appreciate quality and enjoy indulgence.

The name 'Shovel & Bell' came from the idea of traditional gelato shovels and the childhood feeling of hearing the ice cream bell. Manic Design introduced a color palette of 10 gelato-inspired colors, along with gelato drips and splatters as part of the visual elements. While they wanted the brand to reflect quality and luxury, they also wanted to bring out the childish side in people — the feeling of a cold scoop on a hot summer day.

Design Agency: Manic Design
Creative Direction: Karen Huang
Art Direction: Adeline Chong
Design: Jenny Ji Jun, Wong Chee Yi
Illustration: Elizabeth Sutrisna

'wich

'wich is the first concept sandwich shop in Hong Kong. It offers a unique variety of gourmet sandwiches to suit customers' varying tastes and appetites over the course of the day. Homemade soups, freshly prepared salads, delicate espresso drinks and fine wine by the glass are also served to complement the 'wich experience. They are simply sumptuous works of art — a delight to customers' eyes and taste buds.

BLOW was asked to create the visual identity and packaging system for 'wich. To project the sophisticated image of a high quality gourmet sandwich, they developed a visual identity with a cool color tone. Also, a series of ingredient icons were created to form the look and feel. The master design was applied to all in-store collaterals, including the packaging system, uniforms for chefs and waiters, the signage system and environmental graphic.

Design Agency: BLOW
Creative Direction: Ken Lo
Design: Ken Lo, Crystal Cheung, Caspar Ip
Illustration: Crystal Cheung
Photography: Brian Ching

Micheline Interior

Micheline is a printing boutique that was founded in the mid 1970's. Back then, it was very uncommon to find a print shop that offered both design and high-end printing under the same roof. The boutique came to Anagrama because they needed their brand and store to express uniqueness, elegance and modernity.

The space is inspired by the ambiance of print-shops in the seventies. It has a few contemporary accents such as the lighting, which gives the interiors a vanguardist atmosphere. Anagrama made sure to use a neutral color palette, focusing all of the attention on the shelves holding the printing catalog and emphasizing the brand's presence.

This project was developed with the collaboration of German Dehesa and Roberto Treviño.

Design Agency: Anagrama

Micheline Branding

Micheline is a printing boutique founded in the mid 1970's. Back then, it was very uncommon to find a print shop that offered both design and high-end printing under the same roof. The boutique came to Anagrama because they needed their brand and store to express uniqueness, elegance and modernity.

Micheline is now a printing boutique of the highest quality. They welcome all generations, making them feel comfortable and in their own environment. Anagrama selected a color palette based primarily on black and white, since all of the printed pieces are very colorful.

They also designed a monogram that would be easy to reproduce on all of their printed pieces and would work as a signature for their workshop.

Design Agency: Anagrama

Nordic House

Nordic House is a yet-to-be-launched dry cleaning shop in San Francisco, California. Anagrama's approach to Nordic House's branding was focused on Scandinavian design; combining simple geometric forms with a clean, sharp, well-distributed logotype and an icy, cold color palette. Snowy white, chilly grey, pine needle green and fresh salmon combine to create a cool Nordic landscape complete with its pure, immaculate and undisguised scents. A few icons are present in the overall identity, designed with a stark and reductionist style that captures the brand's elemental emphasis on honesty, clarity and above all, quality. Apart from their premium dry cleaning services, Nordic House will also sell exclusive, quality items such as scented soaps and undershirts.

Design Agency: Anagrama

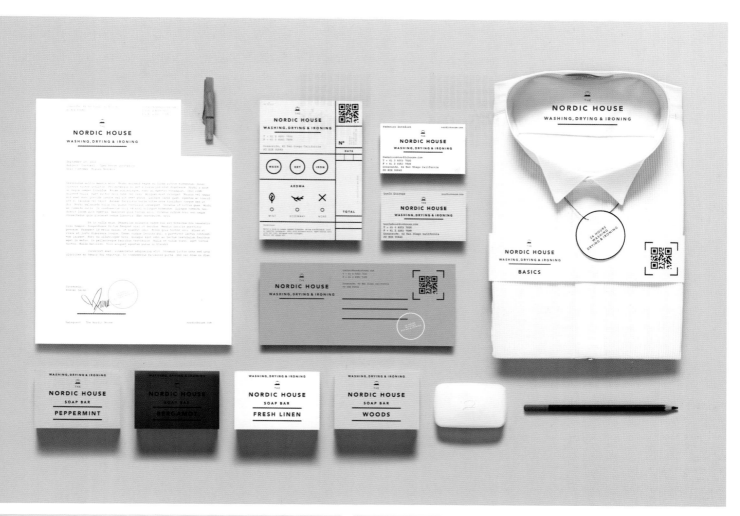

Sukré Salé

In 2012, Cesar Fernández-Bravo and Lucas Gil-Turner were mandated to create from scratch the entire corporate identity, interior design, packaging and communication strategy of a brand new restaurant chain in Bratislava, Slovakia. The idea was to offer handmade natural fast food with delicious recipes from France and Switzerland. Its mission was to bring a healthier alternative to people looking for a quick meal, without sacrificing quality and taste. Having this in mind, a comprehensive scope of services were provided: creation of name, logo, full corporate image, packaging and communication strategy. They were also in charge of the whole restaurant interior design. With the intention to create a logo that represents both the name of the restaurant and the wide selection presented, they played with the geometrical figures of a circle for the pastry and a triangle for the sandwiches, resulting in this very symbolic logo. Sweet and salty simply match!

Branding and Shop Design: Cesar Fernández-Bravo, Lucas Gil-Turner

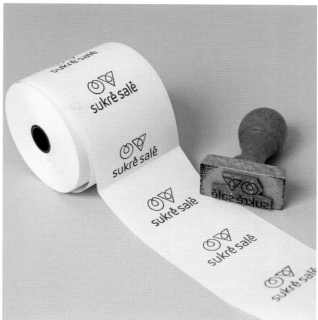
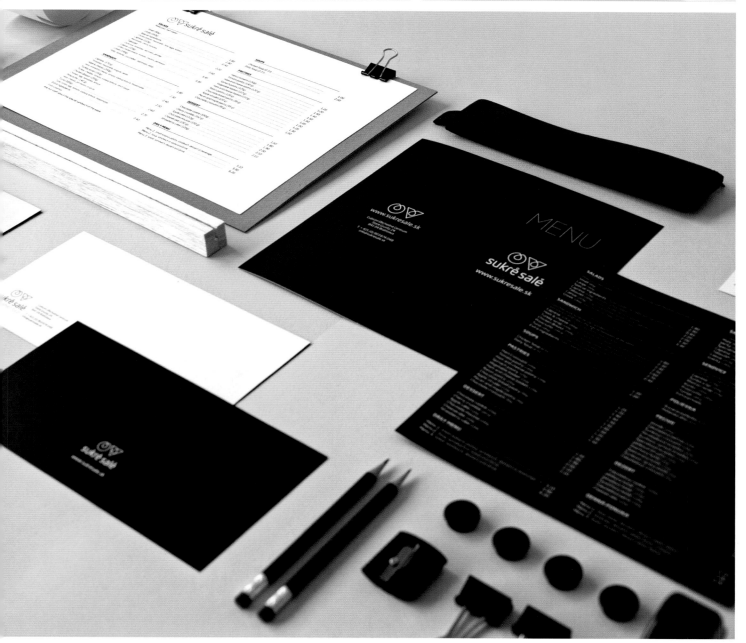

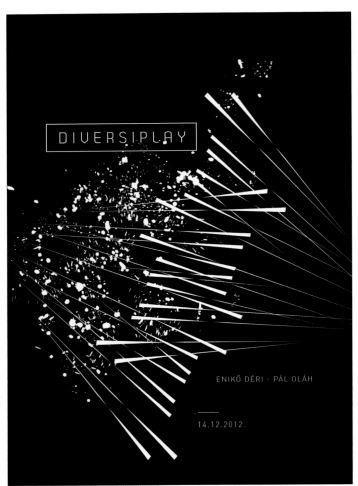

Diversiplay

Diversiplay is an experimental, interactive, application artwork that connects typography with sound and demonstrates the interaction between the two. In the form of an alphabet, we are presented with an audible experience. The typefaces are only connected by their foundation in sound, resulting in a very diverse appearance. The designer's intention for Diversiplay was to create an experience unlike the usual audio visualization, creating instead a completely personal approach. The appearance of every single typeface displays the subjective impression made by the different sounds and noises. The typefaces are the designer's reaction, visual items assigned to sounds.

Design: Eniko Deri, Pal Olah
Programming of the application: Pal Olah
Photography: Laci Kohegyi

My Honey Hair Salon

The project is the concept of a hair salon — a black and white identity and storefront design where the motif of a comb dominates. Aside from using the comb as a pattern, it is the key element of the hair salon with its functional and visual role. The simple logo is the starting point of the hair motif on the windows and it can also be used in other parts of the identity.

Design: Eniko Deri
Concept: Eniko Deri
Photography: Laci Kohegyi

Örkény Festival

The festival was held as part of the memorial year for the popular Hungarian writer Örkény István, the master of grotesque, who lived in the 20th century. The concept was to design a complex festival identity that attempts to express the style of the writer. Eniko Deri used the contrast of black and white with punctuation marks in every detail of the ID.

Design: Eniko Deri
Photography: Laci Kohegyi

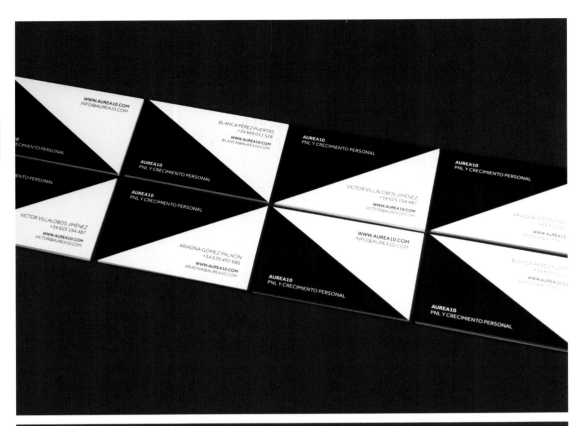

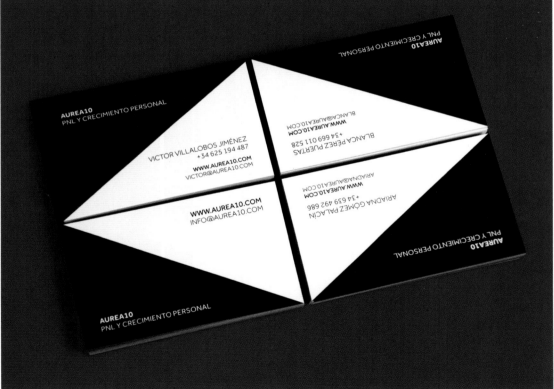

AUREA10

AUREA10 was a project created with the objective of disseminating the experience of its members in the managing of emotions, improving the quality of life and achieving excellence on a personal and professional level.

For the logo, taking as its starting point the letter 'F', there was an experiment with the golden ratio, creating a symbol that aesthetically reflects the essence of the project. The result was a golden rhombus.

The identity is based on the opposition of antagonistic concepts such as force-weakness, stiffness and flexibility. The use of black and white represents this duality.

Design Agency: Porcelain Studio

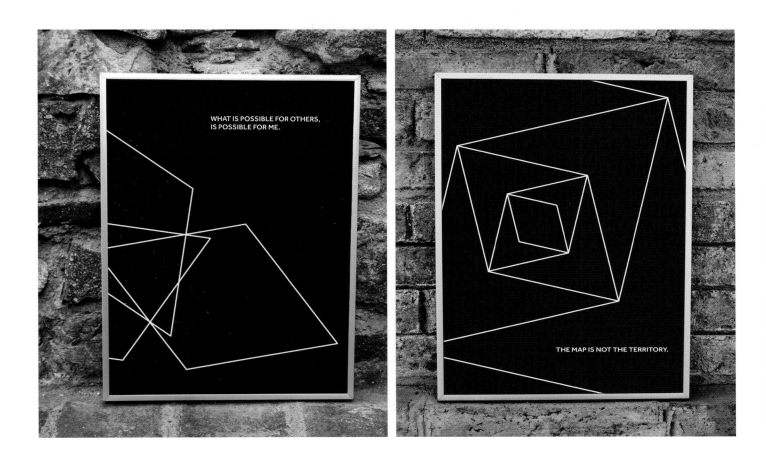

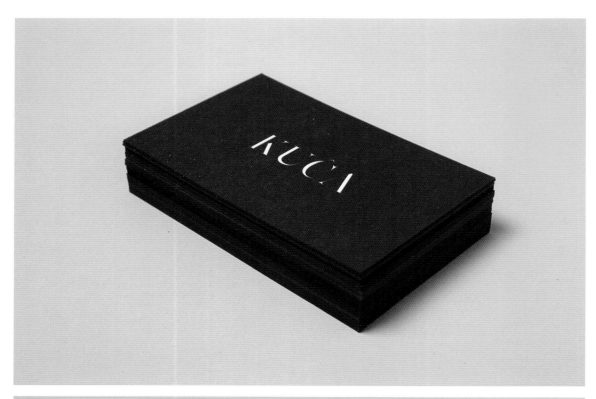

Kuca

Kuca is a design studio that works across the disciplines of architecture, interior and product design. They are committed to delivering exemplary and environmentally responsible architecture, interior and product design with a social, economic and ecological conscience.

Longton created custom typography and a simple color palette, which compliments the work but also enables the work to speak for itself.

Design: Longton

Fieventwentich

Fieventwentich is a fictional soap manufacturer that produces high quality soaps. The soaps
are quadratic and weigh 25g. The name Fieventwentich is Low-German and means twenty-five.
It represents the origin of the factory and the business concept that combines tradition and
modernity. The black paper with a soft finish stands for elegance and the soft surface of the soaps,
while the white uncoated paper supports the handmade and individual character of the brand.
The appearance becomes relaxed by a pattern of squares. The entire design is characterized by the
recurrent form of the square.

Concept/Design/Realization: Janina Dröse

Longton

Like any creative business, one of the most challenging projects is your own identity.
Longton collaborated with creative writer Ennis Cehic to help develop their profile.
Once they figured exactly where they wanted to position themselves, Longton worked
on creating a logo that captured all of their objectives and values.

Design: Longton
Copy Writing: Ennis Cehic

Michael Longton
+61 (0) 422 084 040
michael@longtondesign.com

Longton
Design + Direction

Level 4, 105 Victoria St
Fitzroy VIC 3065 Australia
longtondesign.com

Michael Longton
+61 (0) 422 084 040
michael@longtondesign.com

Longton
Design + Direction

Level 4, 105 Victoria St
Fitzroy VIC 3065 Australia
longtondesign.com

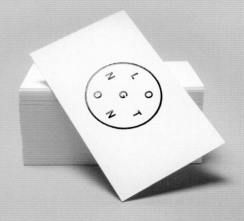

World of Whisky

Bond created the identity for Altia/Wennerco's whisky portfolio named
World of Whisky. The identity follows a no nonsense, straight to the point
approach. Strong black and white graphics are complemented by clever
copy and intricate illustrations.

Design Agency: Bond
Design: James Zambra, Jesper Bange, Tuukka Koivist

State of the Obvious® Collection

With consumerism at an all time high, and brand image playing an ever more important role in consumers buying choices, Mash Creative felt an overwhelming desire to challenge what has become 'The Norm.'

The team believe there is a niche in the market for a collection of products that turn conventional branding on its head. S/O/T/O (State of the Obvious) is a range of merchandise and apparel that does just that. S/O/T/O uses the products description to create a unique brand identity.

The S/O/T/O collection is designed to have a playful, modern and bold brand image that is flexible enough to be adapted across a wide variety of items. The collection will continue to grow, with many other products already in the pipeline.

Design: Mash Creative

Boxpark

Boxpark's vision for creating a 'community of brands' — a temporary collection of shops, cafes and galleries — out of shipping containers was an exciting new concept. Set in Shoreditch, East London, an area known for a distinctly leftfield approach to retail, Boxpark aimed to raise the bar in one of the world's most creative markets.

StudioMakgill created a strong visual identity with an industrial aesthetic, reflecting the monolithic quality of the containers themselves. They designed not only the identity, website and brochures, but also managed the design and production of the directional signage, London-wide advertising campaigns and large format graphics. They continue to provide ongoing design support.

Design Agency: StudioMakgill
Architect: We Like Today
Photography: Archard Architectural

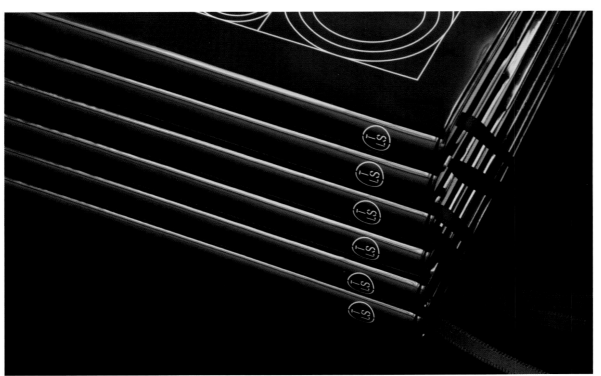

The Lollipop Shoppe

StudioMakgill were asked to help The Lollipop Shoppe take its next step: to create an identity built on innovation, personality and refined aesthetics.

Set up as a shop designed to showcase furniture and accessories in a way that was at once relaxed, informal and forward looking, The Lollipop Shoppe was keen to transform this early success into a brand known for its attention to detail, an approach that conveys passion, originality and taste — all in the name of good design. In doing so, it set out to make its mark in a seriously competitive market.

StudioMakgill wanted to create something that reflected the heritage of their large line of classic products from manufacturers like Vitra, something that also fit in with contemporary brands like Established & Sons and conveyed the straightforward nature with which The Lollipop Shoppe conducts its business. They created a bespoke stencil typeface (partly inspired by the 20th century modular stencils created by Josef Albers and Le Corbusier, but with a contemporary elegance) that is used throughout the identity.

Design Agency: StudioMakgill
Interior: Found Associates

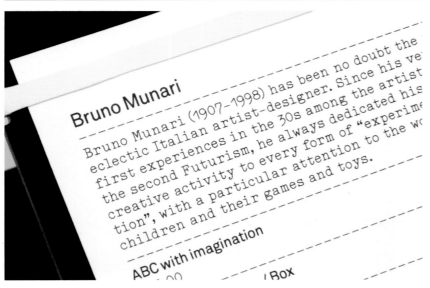

Space Explore

Teaching kit for a space club. Through this teaching kit, the audience learns more about outer space and constellations, such as how to find the star in the star map and stargazing. The concept of this teaching kit is camping in space. When audiences use this kit, they get together with friends and explore unknown knowledge about outer space.

Design: Fundamental

Stage01
Getting Start

A pair of bright eyes, a small f lashlight covered with red cellophane and a star map are all you need. Binoculars is a plus but not a must.

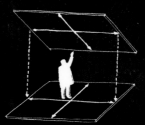

Stage02
Magic of a star map

Rotary star map is best for beginners, while monthly star map usually gives more details of the night sky.

20°

Stage03
Starry starry nights

Spotting a constellation with star maps is similar to locating yourself in the field with a terrestrial map. You have to take the bearings, understand the scale and then look for any prominent stars.

10°

Stage04
How to use the Digital Camera to take the nebula's photo?

Digital camera nowadays is capable of many aspects in astrophotography. The simplest way is to mount your camera on a tripod and exposure as long as your camera permits. (Recent digital cameras support exposure as long as 1 minute)

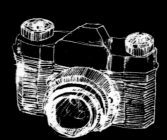

The 🚀
Space
explore

everyone can be the space explorer

Otley Brewing Company

Beer evolution is the mantra at Otley — a synergy of passion, innovation and fresh attitude that results in non-conformist, progressive brews for independently minded free thinkers and drinkers.

Smörgåsbord's brief reflected this and challenged them to break away from the hackneyed and traditional beer or 'real ale' branding. Out went the supposed witty associations to mythical beasts and forest animals and in came a utilitarian yet elegant look and feel that reflected the quality and purity of the brew.

Concept/Creative Direction: Smörgåsbord

THE TROPHY CABINET

Year	Competition	Beer	Category	Award
2005	South Devon CAMRA Beer Festival	Experiment-O	Strong Ale	Runner up
2006	SIBA West Regional Beer Festival	DARK-O	Milds	Bronze
2006	Great Welsh Beer and Cider Festival	O1	Golden Ales	Gold
2006	Great Welsh Beer and Cider Festival	OG	Strong Ales	Gold
2006	Great Welsh Beer and Cider Festival	O8	Barley Wines	Gold
2006	Great Welsh Beer and Cider Festival	O8	Overall Champions	Gold
2006	Great Welsh Beer and Cider Festival	OG	Overall Champions	Bronze
2007	Great British Beer Festival	O1	Golden Ales	Bronze
2007	SIBA Wales and West Regional Festival	O8	Strong Ales	Gold
2007	SIBA Wales and West Regional Festival	O2	Best Bitter	Gold
2007	SIBA Wales and West Regional Festival	O2	Overall Champions	Silver
2007	Leeds Beer Festival (CAMRA)	O8	Overall Champions	Gold
2007	Great Welsh Beer and Cider Festival	O8	Barley Wines	Gold
2007	Great Welsh Beer and Cider Festival	O-GARDEN	Speciality Beer	Gold
2007	Great Welsh Beer and Cider Festival	O-GARDEN	Real Ale in a Bottle	Gold
2007	Great Welsh Beer and Cider Festival	OG	Strong Bitter	Gold
2007	Great Welsh Beer and Cider Festival	O1	Golden Ales	Gold
2008	SIBA National Beer Competition	O2	Champion Best Bitter	Silver
2008	SIBA Wales and West Regional Festival	OG	Strong Bitters	Gold
2008	True Taste Awards	O1	Alcoholic	Reserve Winner
2008	True Taste Awards	O8	Alcoholic	Highly Commended
2008	Great Welsh Beer and Cider Festival	O1	Golden Ales	Silver
2008	Great Welsh Beer and Cider Festival	O8	Barley Wines	Gold
2008	Great Welsh Beer and Cider Festival	O8	Overall Champion	Gold
2008	Great Welsh Beer and Cider Festival	O-GARDEN	Speciality Beer	Gold
2008	Great Welsh Beer and Cider Festival	OG	Strong Bitters	Silver
2008	Great British Beer Festival	O1	Golden Ales	Gold
2008	Great British Beer Festival	O-GARDEN	Speciality Beer	Gold
2009	National Winter Ales Festival	O8	Barley Wines	Bronze
2009	Great Welsh Beer and Cider Festival	O6 PORTER	Overall Champion	Bronze
2009	Great Welsh Beer and Cider Festival	OG	Overall Champion	Silver
2009	Great Welsh Beer and Cider Festival	O6 PORTER	Porters	Gold
2009	Great Welsh Beer and Cider Festival	OG	Strong Bitters	Gold
2009	Peterborough Festival	O8	Barley Wines	Bronze
2010	National Winter Ales Festival	O8	Barley Wines	Bronze
2010	CAMRA Champion Welsh Winter Festival	O8	Barley Wines	Silver
2010	CAMRA Champion Welsh Winter Festival	DARK-O	Stouts	Bronze

Otley Brewing Company Ltd

Unit 42
Albion Industrial Estate
Pontypridd CF37 4NX

+44(0)1443 480555 Tel/fax
sales@otleybrewing.co.uk
otleybrewing.co.uk

CAMRA SAYS THIS IS REAL ALE

OTLEY BREWING COMPANY

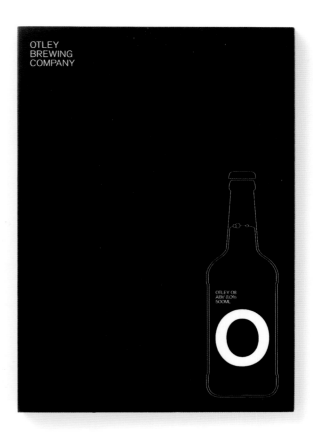

OTLEY
BREWING
COMPANY

One Point Six One Eight

Responding to the content of migration and perfection, Winnie Wu devised a
format that reflected 'no beginning and end' to connote the continuous loop of
migration patterns—an accordion-type book that opens up to reveal a single
spiraling sheet of paper. She wanted the book to be complex inside yet deceptively
simple outside, as a reflection of what perfection really is—how it is achievable
through a mathematical formula and yet never quite achievable in reality.

Design: Winnie Wu

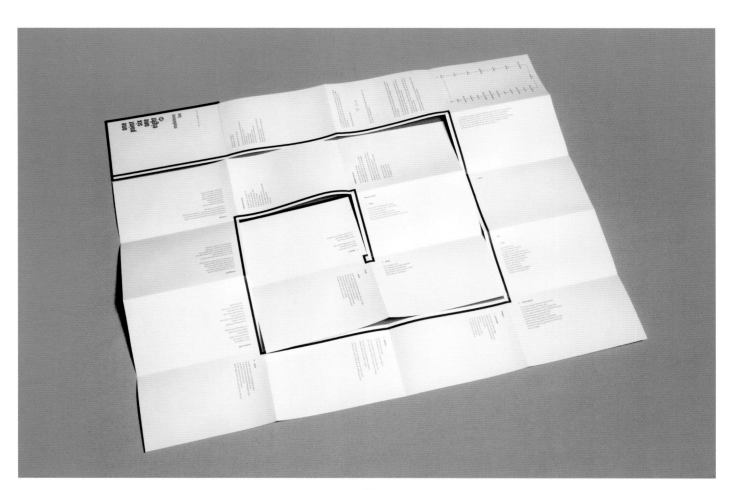

ANKER'T Ruin Bar

The widely known Hungarian Anker Club's summer version is ANKER'T. It's an open air space, which was launched in June 2012. The basic idea of the ANKER'T was to create a unique place with a minimal design. The aim of the owners was not to be just one of a thousand bars located in historic building ruins in Budapest. Gergely Szoke used only two fundamental colors, black and white, for the design and paired it with playful typographic choices. What gives the interior a little twist are the light-boxes, which direct guests' focus to the walls.

Design: Gergely Szoke

Winecast

Winecast is an online wine-tasting, curating and delivery service based in The Netherlands. After taking a 'taste test' that takes likes, dislikes, tastes and habits into account, Winecast presents the user with a personalized (and further customizable) selection of six wines to be sent every month for a fixed fee. Anagrama's proposal began with the naming: Winecast sends a selection, or cast, of 6 bottles optimized to the user's tastes, much like actors selected for a play based on their aptitudes for a precise role. It could also be thought of as a cast molded specifically after a person's preferences.

Their design explores the visual world of post and parcel packaging. The perforations or rippled edge found in the stationery and the box labels were inspired by the characteristic appearance of a postage stamp.

Design Agency: Anagrama

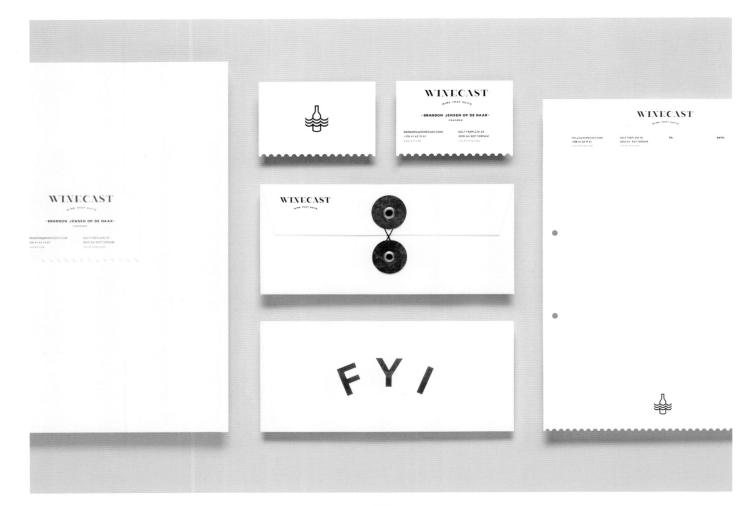

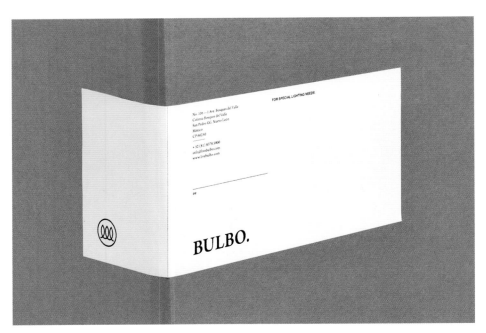

Bulbo

Bulbo is a lighting boutique specializing in premium points of purchase.

Their added value relies on the fact that each of their pieces is carefully selected from their catalog and their ability to manage an entire lighting project for a specific space.

When it came to their identity, Bulbo knew the importance of portraying their products' sophistication.

They approached Anagrama asking for a brand identity that communicated the brand's elegance above anything else.

The monogram is inspired by the language of electric diagrams and it is complemented with a sober serif typeface.

Design Agency: Anagrama

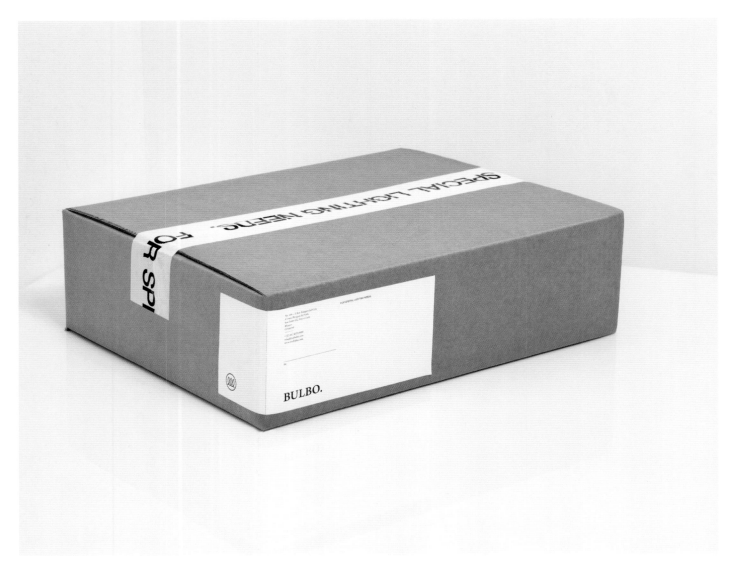

Sincerely Yours,

Sincerely Yours, is a self-initiated graphic design exhibition set up by Solene Leblanc with eight other recent graduates from the London College of Communication's 2011 Master of Arts Graphic Design course. They worked collaboratively to design and produce the show's visual identity, communication materials and exhibition design.

Design: Elisabeth Bolzon, Emmanuelle Goutal, Albane Jerphanion, Marwan Kaabour, Solene Leblanc, Kwong Li, Laia Sacares, Leif Steen and Sophia Stupperich

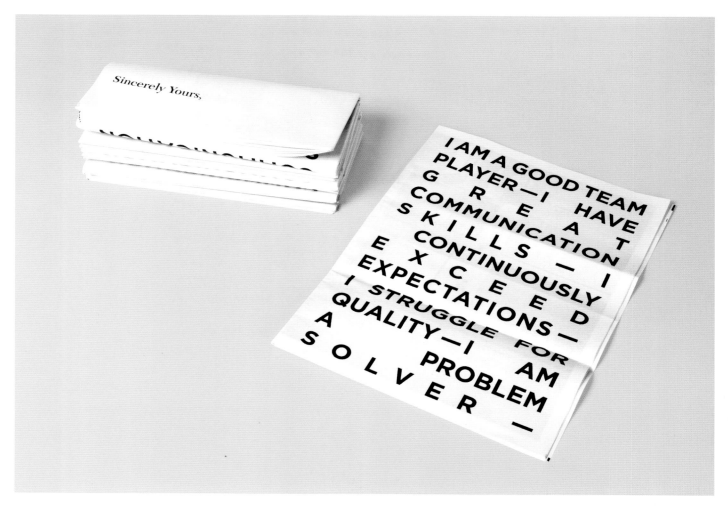

Lupains

21 recipes for grain bread destined for craftsmen bakers could not be more of a beautiful inspiration. The mill company of Bachasson asked Les Bons Faiseurs to design the new visual identity for the brand Lupains. The grains displayed, as if in a herbarium, illustrate each recipe in a very precise and poetic way, creating a strong and at the same time, clear visual identity.

Design Agency: Les Bons Faiseurs
Creative Direction: Etienne Rothe
Art Direction: Fanny Katz

LUPAINS
MAXI FIBRES

LUPAINS
TOURNESOL

LUPAINS
TROIS GRAINES

LUPAINS
DES GRAINES, DES MAINS, DES PAINS

LUPAINS
MAXI FIBRES

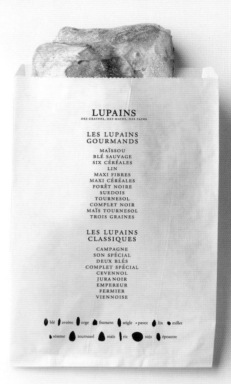

LUPAINS
DES GRAINES, DES MAINS, DES PAINS

**LES LUPAINS
GOURMANDS**

MAÏSSOU
BLÉ SAUVAGE
SIX CÉRÉALES
LIN
MAXI FIBRES
MAXI CÉRÉALES
FORÊT NOIRE
SUEDOIS
TOURNESOL
COMPLET NOIR
MAÏS TOURNESOL
TROIS GRAINES

**LES LUPAINS
CLASSIQUES**

CAMPAGNE
SON SPÉCIAL
DEUX BLÉS
COMPLET SPÉCIAL
CEVENNOL
JURA NOIR
EMPEREUR
FERMIER
VIENNOISE

blé • avoine • orge • froment • seigle • pavot • lin • millet
sésame • tournesol • maïs • riz • soja • épeautre

LUPAINS
DES GRAINES, DES MAINS, DES PAINS

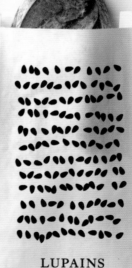

LUPAINS
TOURNESOL

LUPAINS
TROIS GRAINES

Burger Station

Redesign of the logo and packaging for a new chain of burger shops for km 0.

Nueve estudio first received the name Saigon Burger. The Asian reference didn't make much sense when linked to a km 0 concept, so Nueve estudio recommended changing the name to one that was more in line with their type of business.

It was proposed that the new name, Burger Station, was linked to the graphic universe of underground stations. A research study was then carried out in order to pick up the most common and representative references of underground stations.

Design Agency: Nueve estudio

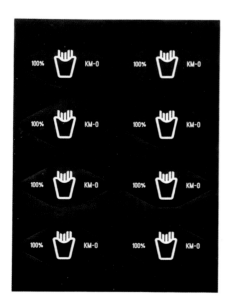

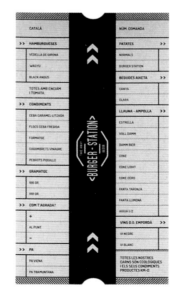

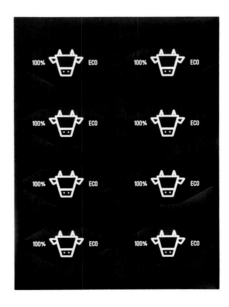

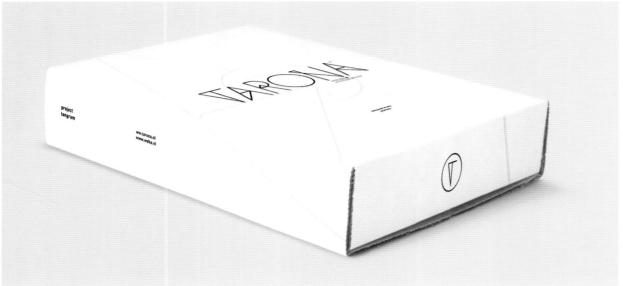

Tarona

Tarona is a photographer based in Rotterdam, the Netherlands. Her work mainly revolves around the conpcet of including the viewer in her journey - in which she aims to discover and capture the moment in between, through the means of portrait, fashion and cinematic photography. Another Day was happy to brainstorm and create the new visual identity for this young and talented photographer. The concept reflects the visual and conceptual journey of Tarona. Taking a detour during your journey can make you discover beautiful, unexpected situations or images.

Design Agency: Another Day
Photography: Tarona Leonaroa

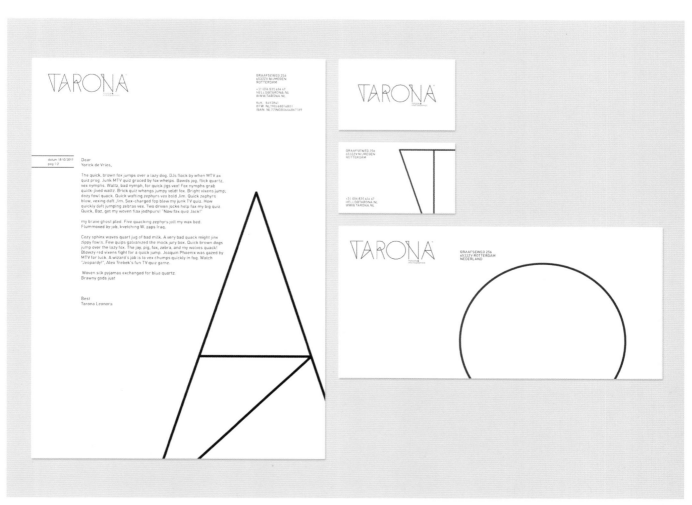

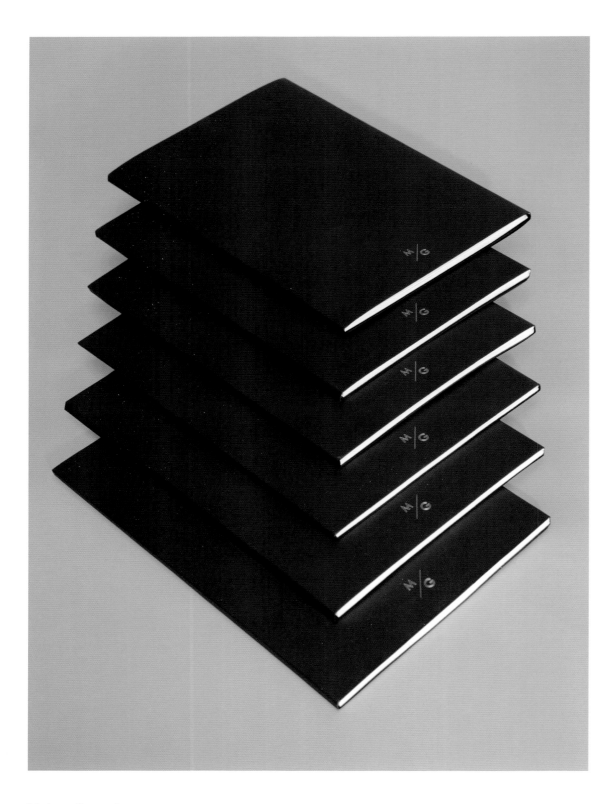

Maison Gerard

Founded in 1974, Maison Gerard is a gallery that specializes in Fine French Art Deco furniture. For the opening of their new gallery showroom, Mother Design created a logo/identity system with corresponding printed materials that communicated the brand's storied elegance, yet contemporary edge.

The new brand expression is used to promote the collections with a premium sensibility, using only the highest quality materials. Each individual piece of design/collateral is created to be a fine collectible artifact in of itself, one worthy of the discernable taste of Maison Gerard's clientele.

Agency: Mother Design
Creative Direction: Michael Ian Kaye, Christian Cervantes
Design: Chris Rogers
Mother: Akiko Kurematsu, Bridie Picot, Julia Reisen
Art Buyer: Bridie Picot, Shalini Carbone
Photography: Josh Dalsimer, Robert Levin

151

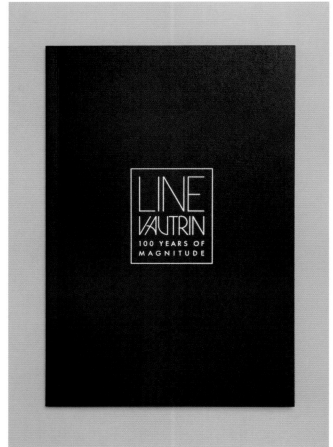

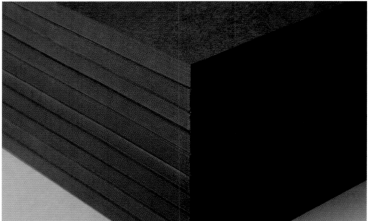

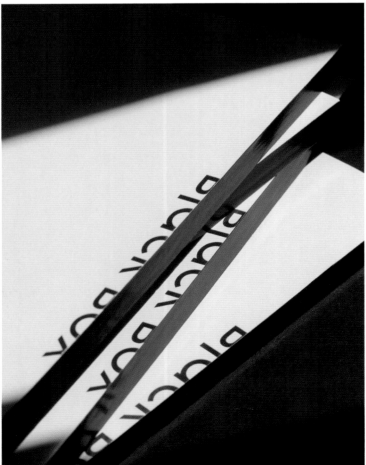

Black Box

Paprika was commissioned to create a new identity related to the opening of this photographer's studio. They played on reflection effect with the logo's symmetry. The black and white identity is the mirror of the theme here: the photography.

Agency: Paprika
Art Direction/Design: René Clément
Creative Direction: Louis Gagnon

Philippe Dubuc Business Cards and Leaflet

Paprika was commissioned to create business cards for a famous cloth designer. The business cards, when placed all together in a pile, form a tablet like shape and appear as black and white pin stripes. This assimilated to the designer's style — simple but spectacular.

Agency: Paprika
Art Direction/Design: René Clément
Creative Direction: Louis Gagno

Simplicim Business Cards and Brochure

Simplicim signature is based on the points assimilated to implantology in dentistry. Paprika developed an identity that is far from what dentists do, thus they created a more graphical approach.

Agency: Paprika
Art Direction/Design: René Clément
Creative Direction: Louis Gagno

Catalina Fernandez

Catalina Fernandez is a high-end pastry boutique established in San Pedro, Mexico.

The concept in which the store's interiors were based is the brand's origin. It began in 1988 as a home-based bakery and ended up as a successful pastry shop.

In order to give the store a look similar to a warehouse/kitchen, Anagrama used packages of sugar, flour and yeast and placed them all over the store. To benefit from the stores tall ceilings, they designed a vertical structure with shelves above the refrigerators. The brick wall with white enamel is meant to make the store look impeccable, but also old fashioned, so there would be an interesting contrast between the worn out bricks and the modern furnishings, with simple and geometrical shapes.

The goal was to create a place that even 20 years from now would still capture the eye of people walking by, with its imposing lighting and simple props.

Design Agency: Anagrama

FUNDADO DESDE 1938

CF

CATALINA FERNÁNDEZ

TALLER REPOSTERO

Cathrine Hammel

Thanks to her grandfather, who was a teacher at the Bauhaus, Catherine Hammel became a designer. Part of her collection is permanent and her goal is to increase those favorites in the collection, thus achieving a timeless quality to the pieces.

A key point was that the identity should work as a platform, which could house collaborations with different art forms.

Olssøn Barbieri articulated the three c's of her philosophy: Comfortable Contemporary Classic.

Inspired by the rationalist geometric design of the Bauhaus school and the drive for the essentials, they created a mark with floating geometrical shapes to manifest both the functional component of her research and the archetypal connotation of her collection.

The three shapes also function as internal departments: Art, Clothes and Accessories.

The font Gill Sans is used with only capital letters and large spacing across the various applications, supporting the idea of reducing to the essentials.

Design Agency: Olssøn Barbieri
Design: Henrik Olssøn, Erika Barbieri
Photography: Sigve Aspelund, AJBstudio

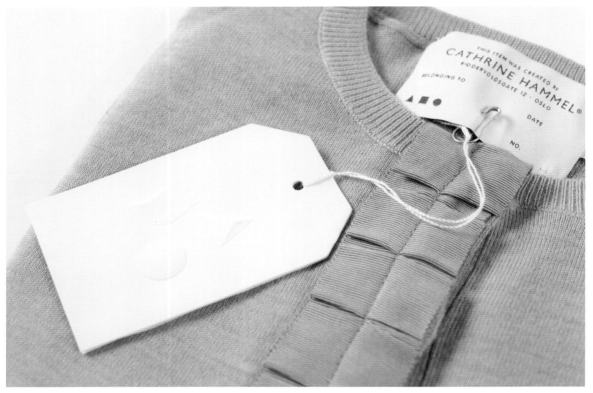

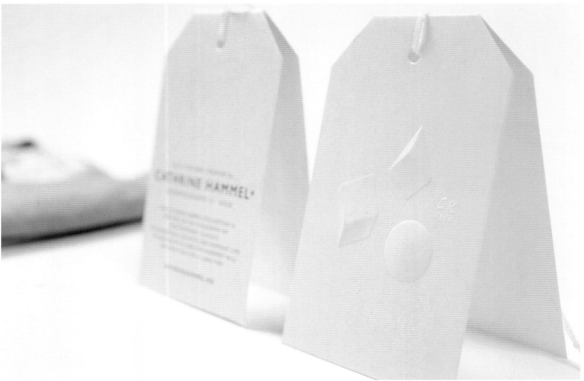

Hecker Guthrie

Paul Hecker and Hamish Guthrie have produced some of the best interiors in the world. When they decided to upgrade their brand to reflect the evolution of their business, Cornwell created an identity not unlike their projects: crafted, detailed, textural, bold, tactile and sumptuous.

Design Agency: Cornwell

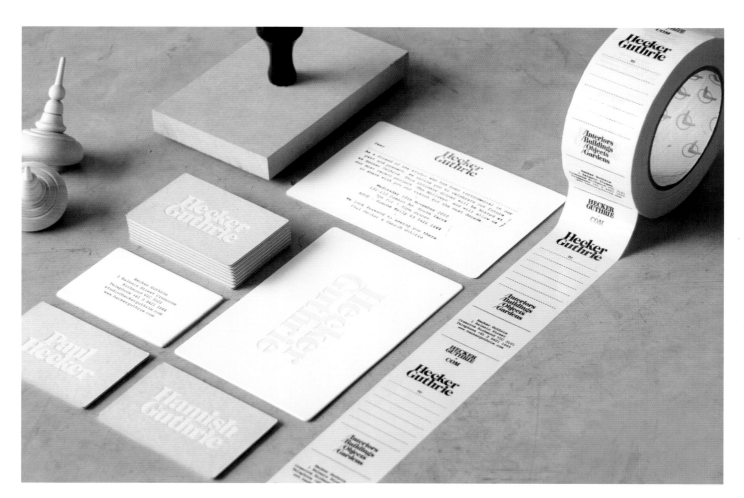

charity: ball Invitation Suite

An elegant but exciting invitation suite for the annual charity: ball.

Design: Mike Smith
Printer: Scott McClelland

Uzuri Makeup Collection

Uzuri is a premium makeup brand, using 100% natural organic ingredients and appealing to the increasing number of women who desire high-quality products with the added benefits of natural ingredients and an ethical guarantee.

Having created a clean confident logotype and brand identity, a full packaging range was developed. Inspired by optical illusionary art, a series of monotone patterns were produced. These played on the concept that makeup itself can be used to create optical illusions. Once applied, these patterns created a striking and original packaging suite, one bold enough to stand out in the competitive beauty market.

Design: Chloë Galea

Self Promo

Jiani Lu's self-identity branding visualizes the young designer's value for simplicity and functionality through stark visual elements and sharply defined contrasts of black and white. Spot UV coated business cards appear stark and bare at first glance, but with closer inspection, reveal a list of self confessed interests and obsessions. The series is playfully paired with subtle unexpected quirks, from hand bound notebooks to hidden messages.

Design: Jiani Lu

Dreux & Ghisallo

Branding, stationery and packaging for a mobile coffee-vending tricycle. The brand revolves around the patron saint of coffee, Saint Dreux, and the patron saint of cycling, Madonna del Ghisallo. It is the intersection of Dreux and Ghisallo that is explored in the customized ampersand found in the logo.

Design: John Wegman
Branding Assistance: David Wegman

Fifty North

Fifty North is a converted warehouse studio based at 50 North St, Richmond, Melbourne. It was co-founded in August 2012 by brothers David and John. The concept of Fifty North was born through the desire to engage and facilitate a communal creative energy. It is home to a wide variety of creative professionals. The brand is simple and clean with a subtle reference to the compass direction of 50 degrees north, found in the slanted line through the O. This is synonymous with the studio's ideology of progression and constructive discourse.

Design: John Wegman

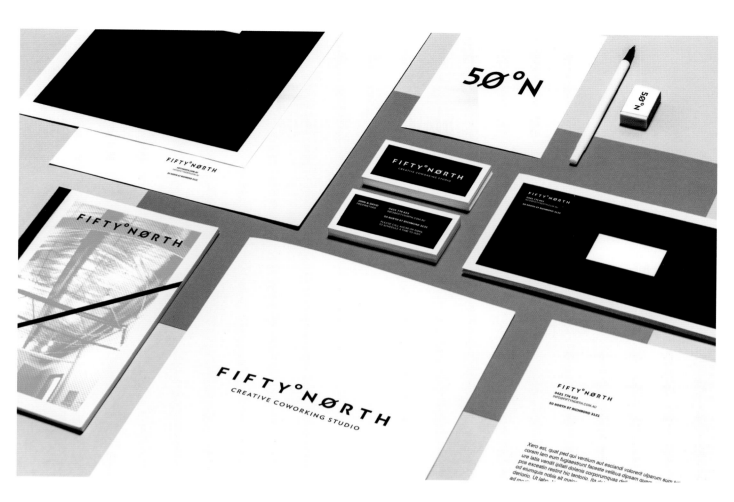

True Colors

Paperlux developed a work and presentation tool for the packaging and cover materials of their cooperation partner and client, Büttenpapierfabrik Gmund paper mill.

Since papers by Gmund are available in a wide range of colors and surfaces, Paperlux decided to keep the design concept as reduced as possible. They limited the design to the basic shapes circle, square and triangle and the colors to black and white. They developed freely combinable patterns and a typography, which also relies exclusively on these elements.

Design Agency: Paperlux
Images: Michael Pfeiffer

Identity and Packaging for Saks Fifth Avenue

Saks Fifth Avenue, the quintessential cosmopolitan retailer, approached Pentagram seeking an all-embracing solution for its visual brand.

The challenges were many: the solution needed to be traditional yet contemporary, appeal to men as well as women and somehow project an 'unmistakably Saks' image.

The solution was to revisit one of the calligraphic logos the store had used for much of the last 50 years. Divided up into details, the newly redrawn logo immediately becomes bold and modern. Every part contains a reminder of the whole, creating a visual language that can be used to unify everything from shopping bags to storefronts and interiors.

Agency: Pentagram
Design: Michael Bierut

Saks Fifth Avenue "Think About..." Campaign

For their 2010 spring campaign, Saks Fifth Avenue introduced a new tagline, "Think about...," — a playful suggestion that shoppers consider new ways to play with their personal style via various items found at Saks. The tagline was finished with amusing statements about fashion and style: "Think about... belting a new tunic with your husband's old tie" and "Think about... making your creative side your outside." If the tone seems a little familiar, it should; the campaign was inspired by the maxims published by legendary fashion editor Diana Vreeland in her "Why Don't You..." column for Harper's Bazaar magazine.

The designers created a witty visual corollary for the campaign. The "Think About..." logo complemented the black and white squares of the Saks Fifth Avenue identity, as well as the right angles and modularity of the identity's grid-based design. Each of the ten letters in "Think About..." was given its own block in the logo. These in turn corresponded to ten individual printed catalogs, each in the shape of its block. The letters on the catalog covers were reversed for fun, creating simple black and white illustrations of collected items, like shoes (the "B," for "Think about...Banning Boring" catalog), watches and jewelry ("K," for "Think about... Karats"), and buttons ("O," for "Think about...Occasionally Outdressing Others.").

Agency: Pentagram
Art Direction: Michael Bierut
Design: Michael Bierut, Jennifer Kinon, Jesse Reed

Think about . . . Banning Boring.

Hotel Daniel Vienna

Simplicity instead of flamboyant excess and fresh ideas instead of awkward hospitality. The hotel's owner, Florian Weitzer, calls it "Urban Stay / Smart Luxury" – perfectly tailored to the needs of the modern traveler. This also applies to the design of the entire hotel, which is the polar opposite of heavy and sedate: simple black and white with a personal touch.

Agency: moodley brand identity
Creative Direction: Mike Fuisz
Design: Sabine Kernbichler
Photography: Marion Luttenberger

Madame/Monsieur

'Madame/Monsieur' or Mrs./Mr. in English, was the branding that was created for the 2012 graphic design exhibition of the graduates of the University of Quebec at Montreal. The exhibition was named as such to evoke the transition between student life and the real world of graphic design work. The 2012 class of designers presented their best projects realized during their three years of university. Now, after the end of the exhibition, they became Mrs. and Mr., ready for the real game. Some goodies and invitations were created for the evening.

Design: Simon Laliberté, Nicolas Ménard, Léo Breton Allaire, Sébastien Paradis, Stéphanie Malak, Valérie Trépanier, Simon L'Archevêque, Aurélien Legall and Jessica Brunner-Gnass

Flock Café

It's all coming together.

Flock Café is a family run establishment that prides itself on freshly made all-day breakfasts and artisanal coffee.

The brand is built upon the concept of 'Coming Together,' assembled primarily using various unique patterns representing different parts of the café.

This allowed Kilo Studio to extend the concept into multiple types of livery such as badges, hand screened aprons and cup sleeves. Most notable would be the name cards, which would be comprised of 3 different designs that would form a larger pattern when pieced together.

Agency: Kilo Studio
Creative Direction: Benjy Choo
Design: Jervic Tan, Lu Jiayi, Angela Thng
Web Programming: Dominique Wong, Glenn Koh

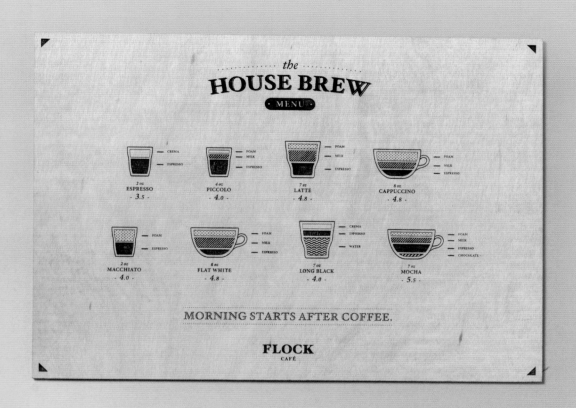

WE ARE DESIGNADDICTED

WE ARE DESIGNADDICTED is a clothing label run by the design studio DESIGNADDICTED.

Design/Art Direction/Photography: Maurice Schilling

Jodin Lamarre Pratte Architectes

Paprika was mandated to create a corporative identity for Jodin Lamarre Pratte Architectes. They wanted an approach that reflected the client: minimalist and timeless.

The monospace fonts were assimilated to construction. They give a structure to the whole project.

Agency: Paprika
Artistic Direction/Design: René Clément
Creative Direction: Louis Gagnon

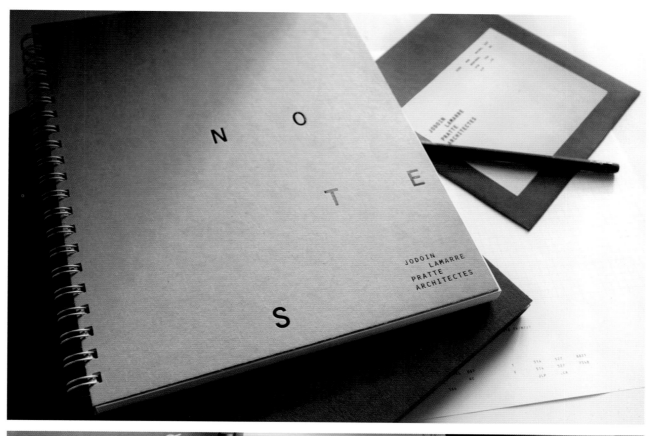

Abeo Design & Architecture Identity

Identity for Abeo, an Australian architecture and interior design studio. The word Abeo means change (metamorphosis) in Latin, so the concept of metamorphosis was crucial in developing the logo. Curvy and round shapes of logotype relates to the dynamic and energetic spirit of the people at Abeo. The latently present infinity symbol communicates Abeo's strive for long lasting principles of originality and good design. Clean, modern and minimal style, together with a black monochromatic color palette, wins the race for Abeo.

Design/Art Direction: Kosta Rakicevic
Creative Direction: Alex Aleksic

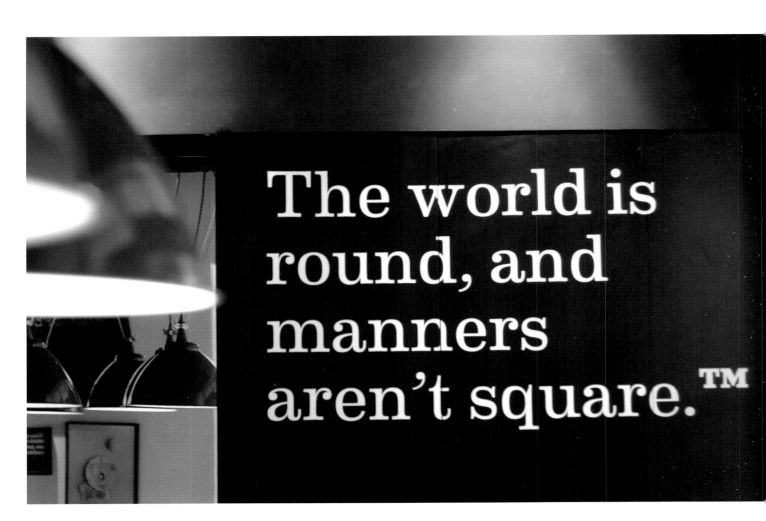

Table Manners

A casual restaurant serving comfort food, Table Manners is the least expected place to hear that phrase. Always staying gracious – but sometimes irreverent – Table Manners promotes proper dining etiquette through engaging and entertaining ways. From the napkins, to the quirky quotes and down to the staff uniform, everything comes with a mischievous twist. The acronymic logo mark of the restaurant secretly hopes to 'trademark' everything it can possibly own.

Design Agency: BLACK
Creative Direction: Jackson Tan
Art Direction: Yong Yi
Writer: Yin Loh, Yong Yi
Illustration: Melvin Tan, Junyao, Yong Yi
Photography: Wong Jing Wei, Yong Yi
Interior Design: Formwerkz

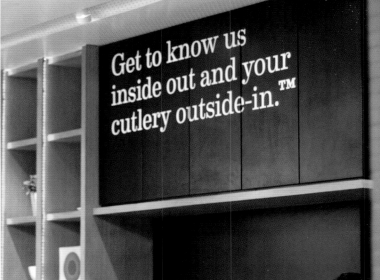

Creation Visual Merchandising (Proposal)

Creation Visual Merchandising specializes in creating unique visual displays for modern retail spaces. This project included identity redesign, branding development and recommendations for this progressive creative business.

As the nature of CVM's work is mostly sculptural in form, a black and white pallet seemed a natural choice for this company's logo and branding. The proposed revamp was intended to produce a modernizing effect by adopting a style that can only be described as a kind of architectural, monochromatic minimalism.

Design: Cindy Forster
Photography: Cindy Forster

LAURIER OUEST AVENUE

Brand development for the Laurier Ouest Merchant Association, a non-profit organization comprising the merchants of the street, defining the area as a rich and cultural destination for visitors of the city of Montreal.

Agency: Paprika
Design/Art Direction: Emanuel Cohen
Creative Direction: Louis Gagnon

Claudia Menrez®

Claudia Menrez® is a talented interior design decorator from Buenos Aires, Argentina. Claudia let herself be inspired by the concepts of late architecture modernism. When Empatía® first contacted Claudia, they were deeply excited about the passion of her work. They decided to create an ultramodernist brand in order to communicate the deco's values. Feelings, forms and color impressions of the designer's work are reflected subtly in the logo, letterhead, business card and website.

The brand imagery, in conjunction with a clean typographic and color palette, creates a powerful and modernist identity. Empatía® also developed a comprehensive set of guidelines, enabling the further development of the brand.

Agency: Empatía®

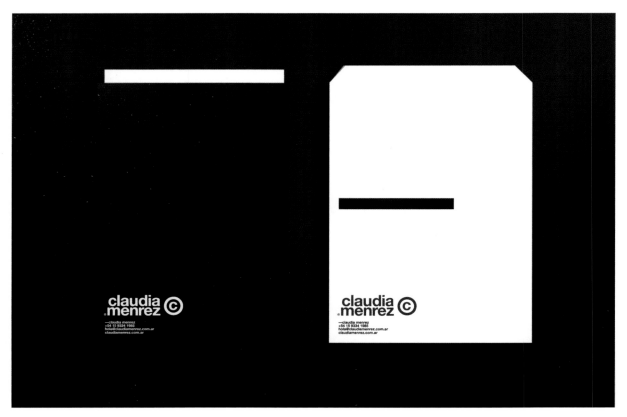

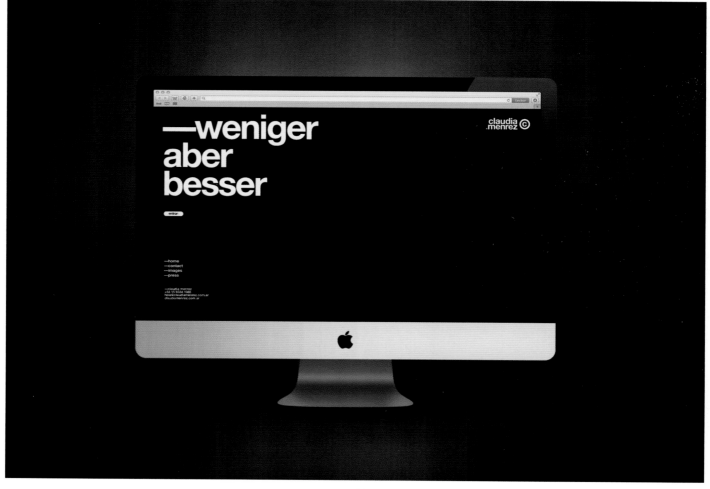

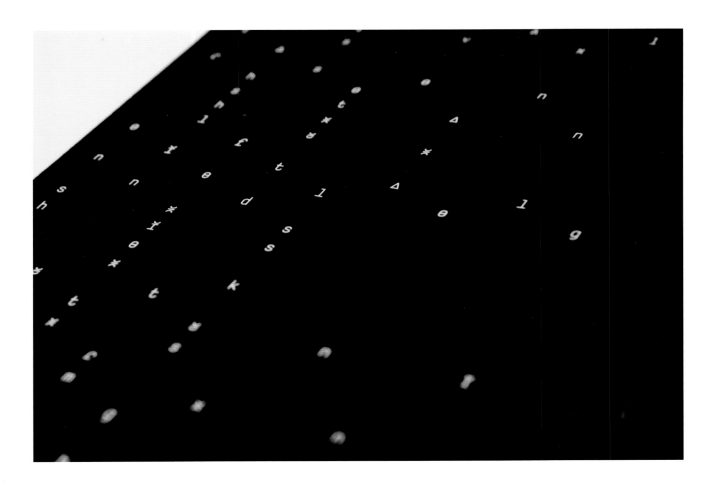

di.natives

di.natives is an IT start-up company that is headed in a new direction. Every employee can decide on what, when, how much or where he/she wants to work. Individuals work autonomously to deliver their part to the company. The corporate design is also simple and clear, yet individual. Each employee has his/her own icons that are on business cards, emails and devices, acting as an individual coding.

Agency: Raum Mannheim

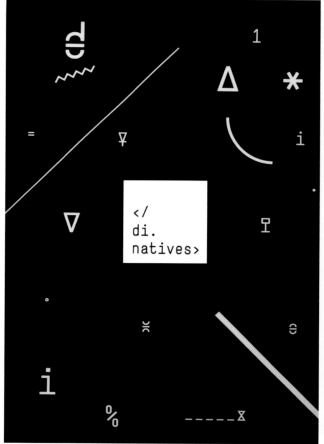

König – Buero fuer Kunst

König Office for Art functions as an interface between artists and the public. They advise artists and organize exhibitions; support those interested in art as well as art collectors. The logo is only revealed in its total form when it is exposed to light.

Agency: Raum Mannheim

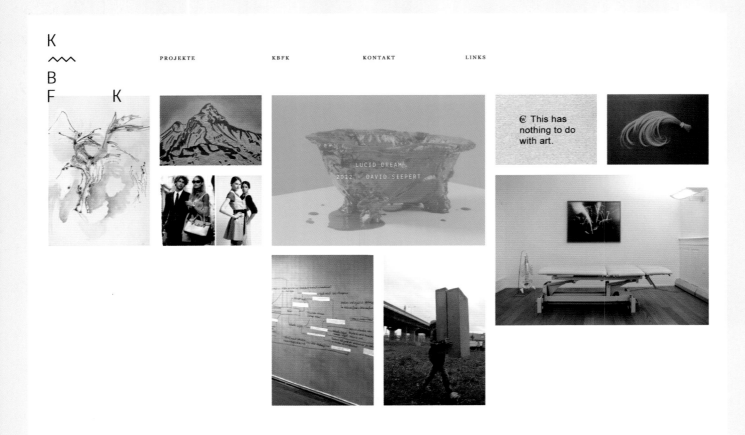

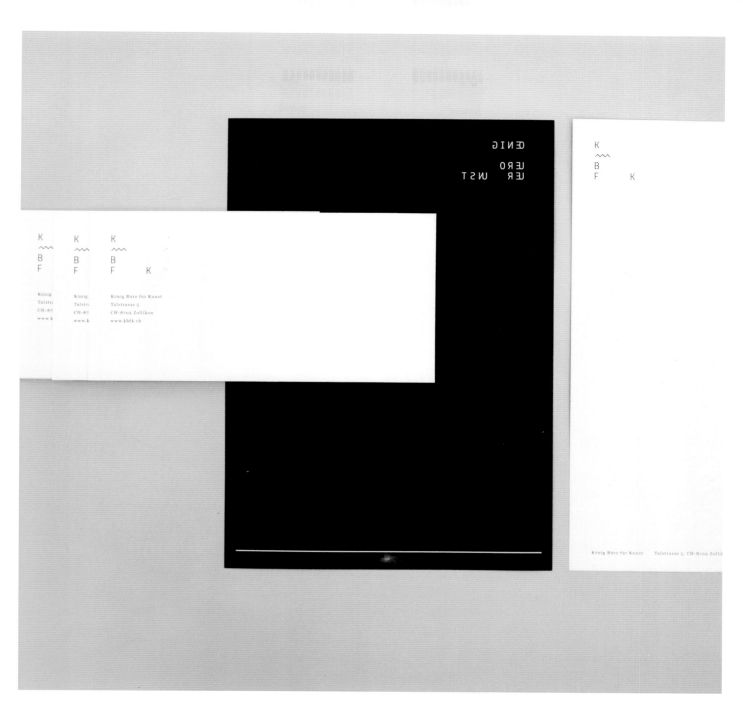

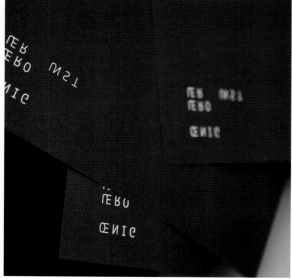

Empatía®

Empatía® is an Argentinian-based design agency operating in a global marketplace. Empatía® is a part of a studio design that seeks to achieve the highest aesthetic, creative and conceptual excellence. They stand for a particular work process. They care for the whole project dimension, since its creative part is essential to its business application. Due to this, they decided to integrate creatives and designers and business and marketing experts.

Empatía® develop print and digital graphics for individuals, companies, art institutions and other organizations around the world.

Agency: Empatía®

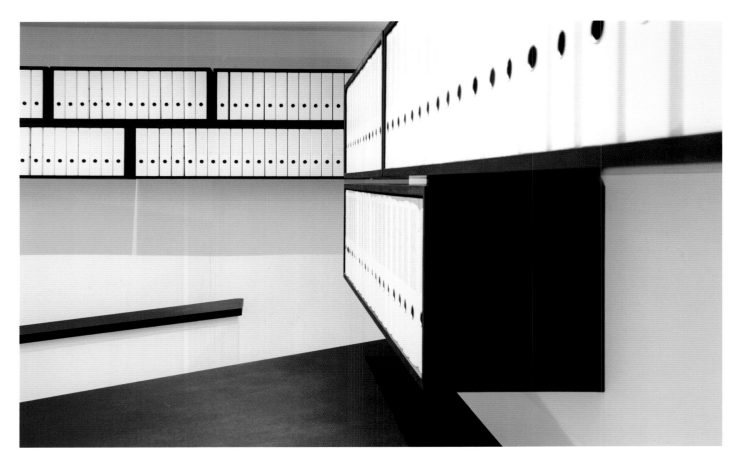

WORL-Anwälte

A plain line without any frills combined with a very airy spacing gives the wordmark a discreet and ageless profile.

The counters and benches' line interferes optically with the room's cubic presence and leads the client directly into the conference room. Color and reduced design refer to the wordmark. The black colored shelves allow for plenty of storage space without overwhelming the room.

Design Agency: LSDK
Creative Direction: Christian Vögtlin
Graphic Design: Michael Adolph
Copywriter: Sergej Grusdew

Andante Hotel

Andante Hotel is an affordable, friendly and comfortable 3 star hotel in the Raval neighborhood of Barcelona.

The branding was built with fonts in black and white to create a modern and clean language.

The speech was very important: positive and friendly messages – this is a responsible and sustainable hotel who care about people and environment – worked together with a pictogram system to build the typographic layouts.

The photo wall murals provide contrast. 20 views shot from different roofs and windows of the city are placed in the rooms to allow the visitors to enjoy the scenario that residents can enjoy every day. For the common areas, the designers used mural photos as well; this time with the approach focused on people.

Agency: Estudio Gerundio
Creative Direction: Lorena Alonso
Design: Lorena Alonso, Abigail Empez
Photography: Ana Madrid (picospardos.net)

No.One Gallery

Branding for an independent commercial art gallery concept, which specializes in photography, illustration and fine art.

Agency: emptypage
Creative Direction: Lukasz Kulakowski

Bach Inspiration Music Learning Center

Brand identity design for a music learning institute. Onion Design used a 'repeat sign' in music notation to represent hard work and patience when people are learning music or musical instruments.

Agency: Onion Design
Creative Direction: Andrew Wong
Design: Charly Chen, Kuan Yu Chen

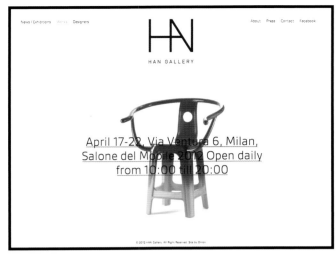

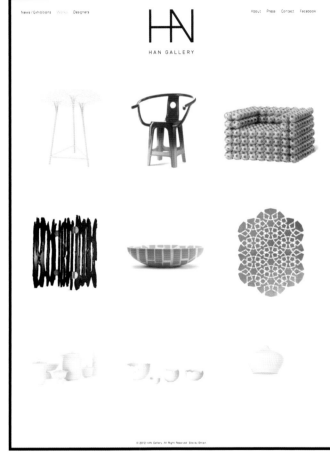

Han Gallery

Building on the success of the design brand 'Yii,' Han gallery moved to an entrepreneurial platform to carry on their research under ex-Droog Design creative director GIJS BAKKER.

The Han Gallery (漢) Logo is a monogram combining 3 characters of their brand name Han.

The geometrical abstraction of the strokes creates ambiguity somewhere between Chinese characters and western writing. When read sideways (right), it resembles the Chinese character (王), meaning 'jade' or 'treasury.'

Agency: Onion Design
Creative Direction: Andrew Wong
Design: Karen Tsai

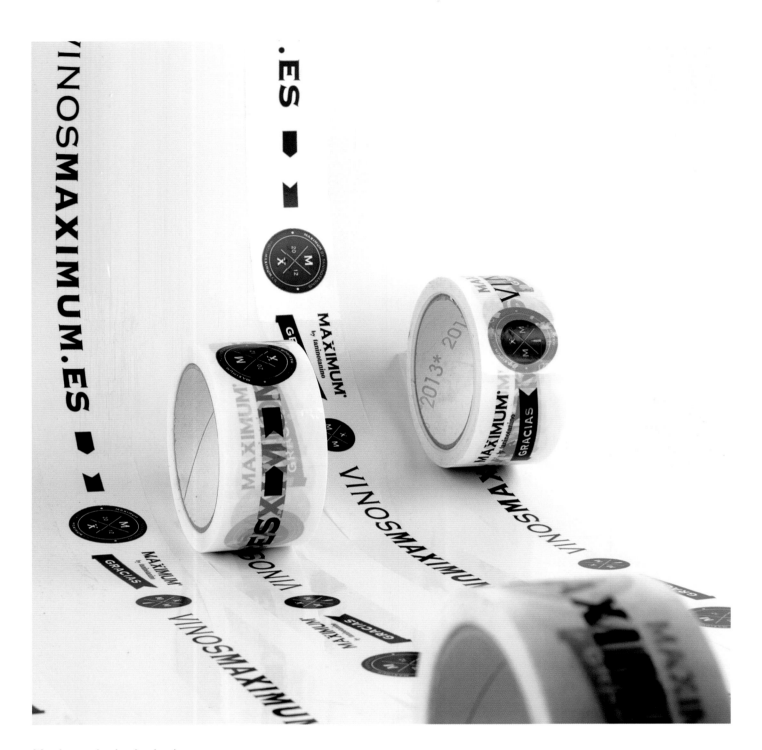

Maximum by taninotanino

Creation and design by Maximum taninotanino® brand, a new online wine shop by Taninotanino Intelligent Wine®.

In creating the concept, the designers took a special interest in the elements and implementation that constitutes the world of wine.

Maximum by taninotanino® has a touch of craftsmanship and the aroma of wine. Rubber stamps, dry wax and paper labels are all elements that rope the rustic charm of this brand together. If we were to compare this brand with a type of wine, it would be a garage wine.

Design: Spaincreative.es

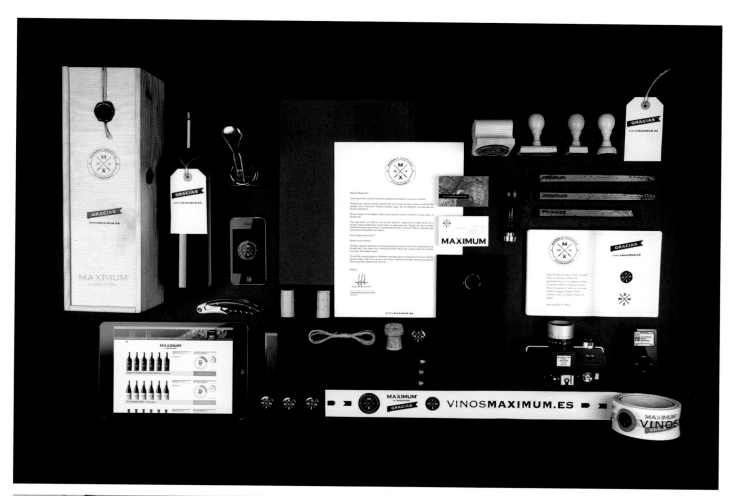

quantum

Architectural and technical lighting Bureau 'quantum' performs comprehensive design of lighting systems for interior and exterior use and is the official distributor in Russia of the Belgian manufacturer of modern innovative lighting solutions 'Deltalight.'

The laconic logo emphasizes perfection and high technology of company. The mission of the company is placed in a succinct slogan 'to the light,' which is played out through the contrast of black and white and the application of UV varnish, creating a vivid reflection of light.

Agency: MYDE
Art Direction/Design: Maxim Yakovlev

Odette Toilette Branding & Packaging

Design Friendship was asked to create a brand identity for Odette Toilette, the perfume lover behind Scratch+Sniff events.

They designed Odette Toilette's identity and stationery along with the first in a series of limited edition wet potpourri launched in collaboration with horticulturalist, Stephen Nelson.

Stylistically, Odette is inspired by vintage French perfumery and the 'O' mark was illustrated to visually reflect the key notes within Odette's favorite scent.

Design: Design Friendship
Illustration: Wendy White

Scissors

An identity redesign project for a Bangkok-based boutique fashion brand called Scissors. Pleat and fold was the main idea behind the design. This unique signature is visible in their clothing design. FARMGROUP decided to subtly emphasize the folding by the manipulation of type and the circle shape. The color selection was simple black and white. It gives a neutral appearance without competing with the actual product, while at the same time giving a mature and mysterious hint to the brand.

Agency: FARMGROUP
Creative Direction: Tap Kruavanichkit
Design: Tap Kruavanichkit, Poomruethai Suebsantiwongse
Photography: FARMGROUP

Size

Identity, branding and web design for an electronic music record label and concert tour based out of Los Angeles, California.

Spearheaded by DJ and veteran producer Steve Angello, Size Records is a powerful contributor of the House and Electronic music scene. About to reach the ten year mark, their image was in need of a little revamping. Along with famous graphic designer Vltranegro, Face was happy to step in.

Face deliberately stepped away from the kind of loud, flashy design usually associated with the genre; they picked strong, respectable fonts to create a bold, timeless and somewhat artsy look. To round everything out they created a smart, memorable logotype to be the centerpiece of the identity: inspired by rhythm, lapses in music production, and yes, size itself.

This project was done in collaboration with Vltranegro.

Design Agency: Face

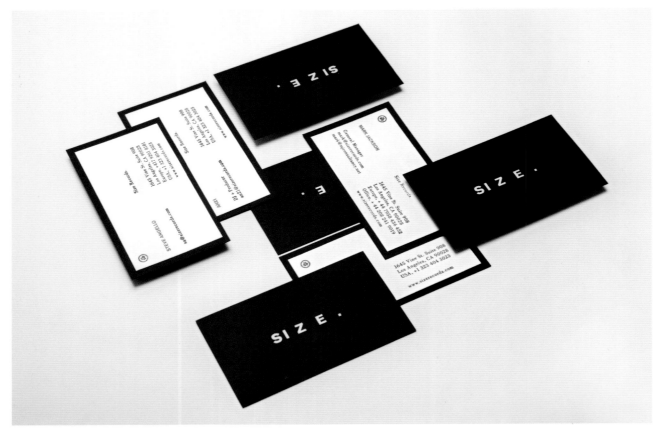

SIZE.

SIZE. RECORDS
info@sizerecords.com
1750 N. Vine St.
Los Angeles 90028
323 462 6252
www.sizerecords.com

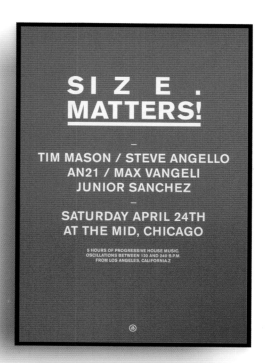

Minus 20° Management

Scandinavia's leading boutique model agency, Minus 20° Management aims its gaze at northern beauty. The Forgery was inspired by runes, the typography of the Vikings and blending in photography by the amazing Victor Eredel. The result became a graphic world full of mystery, eerie beauty and vast Scandinavian vistas.

Agency: The Forgery
Design: Philip Meander
Creative Direction: Dominik Stenberg

Viveka Valentin Jewellery

The jewelry designer, Viveka Valentin has her studio in Cologne. In order to meet the challenge of presenting the diverse materials she uses in her classic and experimental pieces, Raum Mannheim developed a unique visual communication form. The resulting design is therefore multi-faceted, sophisticated and intricate.

Design Agency: Raum Mannheim

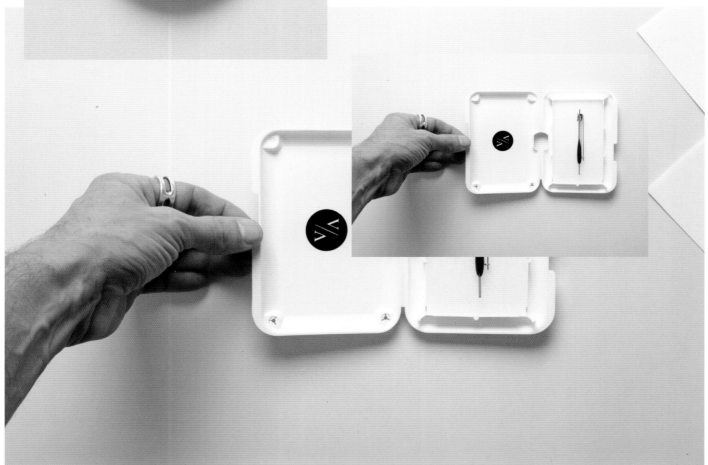

Hoxton Street Monster Supplies

ESTD 1818

~ *Bespoke and Everyday Items for the Living, Dead and Undead* ~

Hoxton Street Monster Supplies

ESTD 1818

~ *Purveyor of Quality Goods for Monsters of Every Kind* ~

Hoxton Street Monster Supplies

ESTD 1818

~ *Purveyor of Quality Goods for Monsters of Every Kind* ~

159 Hoxton Street
London N1 6PJ

TELEPHONE ~ 020 7729 4159

Hoxton Street Monster Supplies

Hoxton Street Monster Supplies was established in 1818, though the exact details of why and by whom, have tragically been lost to history. In 2010, after closing for a much-needed refurbishment, the shop re-opened its doors. The owners pride themselves on being London's only purveyor of quality goods for monsters of every kind. Whether you're a Vampire, Werewolf, Sasquatch or something else entirely, they have everything you need. Hoxton Street Monster Supplies hides a secret doorway to the Ministry of Stories, a volunteering organization that helps young people with all manner of writing through free one-to-one mentoring and writing workshops. All profits from the shop go to the Ministry of Stories.

Design: We Made This

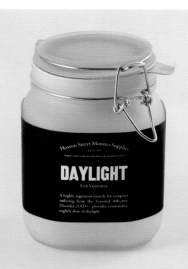

DAYLIGHT
FOR VAMPIRES

A highly ingenious remedy for vampires suffering from the Seasonal Affective Disorder (SAD) – provides a restorative nightly dose of daylight.

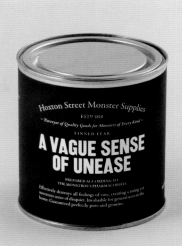

Hoxton Street Monster Supplies
ESTᵈ 1818
~ Purveyor of Quality Goods for Monsters of Every Kind ~
TINNED FEAR

A VAGUE SENSE OF UNEASE

PREPARED ACCORDING TO
THE MONSTROUS PHARMACOPEIA

Effectively destroys all feelings of ease, creating a rising yet uncertain sense of disquiet. Invaluable for general uses in the home. Guaranteed perfectly pure and genuine.

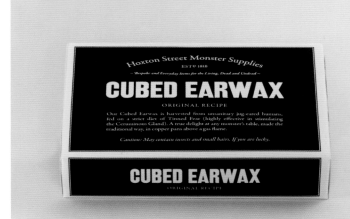

Hoxton Street Monster Supplies
ESTᵈ 1818
~ Bespoke and Everyday Items for the Living, Dead and Undead ~

CUBED EARWAX

ORIGINAL RECIPE

Our Cubed Earwax is harvested from unsanitary jug-eared humans, fed on a strict diet of Tinned Fear (highly effective in stimulating the Ceruminous Gland). A true delight at any monster's table, made the traditional way, in copper pans above a gas flame.

Caution: May contain insects and small hairs. If you are lucky.

CUBED EARWAX
ORIGINAL RECIPE

Hoxton Street Monster Supplies
ESTᵈ 1818
~ Purveyor of Quality Goods for Monsters of Every Kind ~

ZOMBIE FRESH MINTS

Suffering from hideous halitosis after gorging on humans all night? Banish brain-breath with these startlingly strong mints.

SOLD UNDER LICENSE FROM
The Ministry of Stories · www.ministryofstories.org

Hoxton Street Monster Supplies
ESTᵈ 1818
~ Purveyor of Quality Goods for Monsters of Every Kind ~
TINNED FEAR

CREEPING DREAD

PREPARED BY
MR CHARLIE HIGSON

A perspicacious yet plausible remedy that prevents all sense of relaxation. Acts gently and promptly upon the Mind and Emotions. Likely to induce visions of Ghouls, Bogeymen, and Things that go BUMP! in the night.

Hoxton Street Monster Supplies
ESTᵈ 1818
~ Bespoke and Everyday Items for the Living, Dead and Undead ~

IMPACTED EARWAX

White Pike Whiskey

Crafted by a man trained in the Alabama school of fast whiskey, White Pike is a refined spirit made to be shot, sipped or mixed. A recipe of corn, spelt and malted wheat, White Pike is distilled with precision for a smooth stand-alone flavor that mixes in ways brown whiskeys won't.

Highball, flask or straight from the bottle — drink it however and wherever. Not a single ounce of White Pike Whiskey has ever spent more than 18 minutes in prison.

Agency: Mother Design
Creative Direction: Paul Malmstrom, Mark Aver, Blaise Cepis
Design: Peter Karras, Andew Lim, Mark Aver, Kapono Chung, Matt Wenger
Copywriting: Ben Hieger, Laura Perlongo, Peter Karras
Photography: Peter Karras, Blaise Cepis, Mark Aver, Jason Leiva

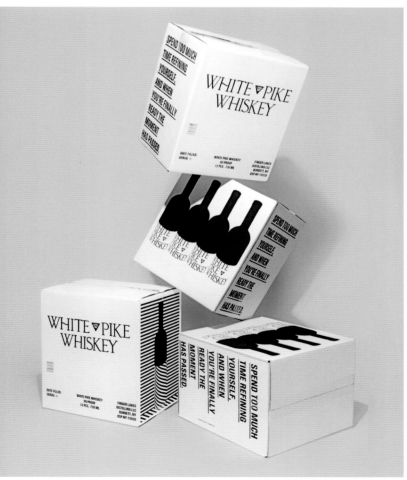

Index

Anagrama
www.anagrama.com

Anagrama is a specialized brand development and positioning agency providing creative solutions for any type of project. Aside from their history and experience with brand development, they are also experts in the design and development of objects, spaces and multimedia projects.
pp.016-017, 066-067, 098-103, 138-141

Another day
www.studioanotherday.nl

Another day is a graphic design studio in the Netherlands. It was founded by Yorick de Vries in 2012. Yorick was born in 1985 in Lelystad, the Netherlands. He now lives and works in Nijmegen. Another day's main focus lies in the fields of art and culture, with a specialization on typography and printed matter.
pp.148-149

Artiva Design
www.artiva.it

Artiva Design is a multi-disciplinary studio dealing in graphic design, branding and visual communication. Based in Genoa, Italy, it was founded in 2003 by designers Daniele De Batté and Davide Sossi.
Their experience covers a wide range of skills in art direction, brand identity, printing, typography, editorial and book design, packaging, exhibition design, digital media, web design and more.
The projects are focused on the presence or absence of graphic elements in geometry and on the use of a rigorous grid system that shows their natural bend towards minimalism.
pp.022-023, 036-039

BLACK
blackdesign.com.sg

BLACK is a multi-disciplinary design practice. Their approach focuses on the creation of value through design. Their sole purpose is to create design ideas that generate social, cultural, commercial, artistic, intellectual and emotional value. BLACK's collaborative process with leading international artists, architects, designers, illustrators, business leaders and institutions allows them to constantly develop interesting and diverse projects that span across branding, graphic design, environmental design, exhibition curation and design, cultural content development, publishing, motion graphics and product design.
pp.192-193

BLOW
blow.hk

BLOW is a Hong Kong-based design studio founded by Ken Lo in 2010. Specialized in branding, identities, packaging, environmental graphics, print, publications and website design, they provide clients with mind-blowing designs in a simple and bold approach that allows the brand to stand out in the crowd.
pp.096-097

Bond
bond.fi

Bond is a creative agency located in Helsinki, Finland, focused on branding and design. Bond was founded and is run by designers who create and renew brands. They work for clients who value creative and practical ideas. They demonstrate their expertise through their work, because design is, first and foremost, a craft for them.
pp.120-121

Brogen Averill Studio
www.brogenaverill.com

Brogen Averill Studio's portfolio comprises major assignments for a 'who's who' of international brands and an enviable selection of niche design projects. Working with some of the world's most successful companies and individuals, they have gained an international reputation, producing versatile and innovative design.
In 2004, after returning from Europe, Brogen Averill Studio was established in New Zealand.
The influence of European design culture and tradition has continued to inform their work, which is applied to a diverse range of mediums, including: brand and identity development, packaging, print, editorial, signage, wayfinding systems and website design and development.
They create concept lead design, investigating requirements and translating them into solutions that are intelligent, creatively inspiring and ultimately different.
pp.044-047

Bunch
www.bunchdesign.com

Bunch is a leading creative design studio offering a diverse range of work, including: identity, literature, editorial, digital and motion. Established in 2002 with an international reach, from London to Zagreb, Bunch has an in-house team of specialists delivering intelligent and innovative cross-platform solutions of communication design. Over the years, many blue chip companies, younger brands and artistic industries have commissioned their services. They have built an impressive client base that covers many styles and disciplines, such as BBC, Nike, Diesel, Sony, Sky, Red Bull and others.
pp.048-053

Bureau Rabensteiner
www.bureaurabensteiner.at

Bureau Rabensteiner is an Austrian design studio that specializes in creative direction and graphic design. The small company structure allows them to work in an inspiring atmosphere, which assures the best results on their clients' projects. The team combines strategic thinking with branding and photography and therefore is able to transport more than just design, but a whole company spirit through different channels. They provide insight into their company life and surroundings. They share the things that inspire them, which emerged as a good way to stay in permanent contact with other designers and interested people all around the world. At the very least, it gives them the opportunity to connect with the right kind of clients, who match their style and thinking and bring interesting new projects and challenges.
pp.054, 060-063

BVD
bvd.se

BVD is a design and branding agency specialized in every physical touch point of a brand in and around a retail environment. Their approach is based on a combination of consumer insight, business focus, ideas and design. They view design as a strategic marketing tool. As such, their primary role is to communicate the brand in a relevant way and to deliver concrete and measurable results. BVD was founded in 1997 by Catrin Vagnemark and Carin Blidholm Svensson.
pp.082-083

charity: water
charitywater.org

charity: water is a New York City-based charity currently working in 20 developing countries around the world, bringing clean water to people in need.
pp.164-165

Chloë Galea
www.chloegalea.com

Chloë Galea is a multi-talented graphic designer and junior art director based in London and Berlin. She has produced elegant design solutions for a wide range of fashion, luxury and lifestyle clients.
pp.166-167

Cindy Forster
www.cindyforster.com.au

Cindy Forster is a professional art director and designer living and working in Sydney, Australia. With a repertoire that spans branding, graphic, catalog and web design along with photographic art direction, Cindy is a multi-disciplinary creative who firmly believes in the power of great design to create great brands. After years spent honing her skills in brand-led design and advertising agencies, Cindy now offers her services to clients directly.
pp.194-195

Cornwell
cornwell.com.au

Cornwell is a creative studio with the depth of an agency. They have the privilege of creating and working with a rich and diverse range of brands. Beyond identity, brand and communications, they look at what is unique to every business they work with and bring the best ideas to the fore. Cornwell collaborate with their clients to develop robust strategic platforms for their brand.
These allow them to create ideas of influence that see people take notice, think differently and change behaviors.
With local, national and global recognition, Cornwell has developed a reputation for excellence. Today, with over 30 professionals with expertise across brand strategy, advertising, design and digital, all of whom bring an insightful and strategic focus to brand-oriented business issues, Cornwell has transitioned from a graphic design studio into a premium brand and communications agency.
pp.163

Daniel Brokstad
www.danielbrokstad.com

Daniel Brokstad is a 24-year-old graphic designer and photographer from Stavanger, Norway. He is currently employed full time at Procontra, but continues to do freelance work in his spare time. Graphic design and photography are not only his work, but also a lifestyle he has chosen to follow. He enjoys doing things a little differently, putting his own style to print, which gives him a good sense of achievement and makes the client happy by having something out of the ordinary.
pp.064-065

Design Friendship
www.designfriendship.com

Founded by Natasha Shah and Chris Hilton, Design Friendship is just that, a friendship born from the love of design. Design Friendship is a small, but perfectly formed studio with over 25 years combined experience on creative projects that stretch from corporate identities, through to Pan-European campaigns for some of the worlds' biggest brands. As the name suggests, Design Friendship is all about creating exciting and lasting friendships with their clients.
pp.219

DESIGNADDICTED
www.designaddicted.de

DESIGNADDICTED is a German design studio with a focus on branding, editorial design, creative direction and textile design. Founded in 2011 by the Hamburg-based designer Maurice Schilling, DESIGNADDICTED loves to create clean and strong design with a passion for typography and handmade items.
pp.186-187

Emanuel Cohen
www.26lettres.com

Montreal based multidisciplinary graphic designer Emanuel Cohen specializes in branding, typography, web/UI and art direction. He develops ideas and effective communication solutions and is currently working full-time for the firm Paprika – though always interested in collaboration and special projects.
pp.196-197

Empatía®
www.helloempatia.com

Empatía® is an Argentina-based design agency operating in the global marketplace.
Empatía® seeks to achieve the highest aesthetic, creative and conceptual excellence. They stand for a particular work process. They care about the entire project dimension, from its creative part to its business application. Because of this, they decided to integrate creative and design and business and marketing experts.
Empatía® develops print and digital graphics for individuals, companies, art institutions and other organizations around the world.
pp.198-199, 204-205

End of Work
www.endofwork.com.au

End of Work is a Sydney-based branding and design consultancy specializing in intelligent, strategically sharp design solutions.
It is their belief that brilliant ideas are the lifeblood of successful businesses. As a result, they are in constant pursuit of solutions that distinguish clients' brands in the marketplace, enhance value and change the way people think.
For every idea they generate, they find an elegant and meaningful form of delivery. These range from the printed page, to the digital and physical environment, but every one has a common thread – their trademark obsession with beautifully crafted visual communication.
pp.014-015

Eniko Deri
www.behance.net/enikoderi

Eniko Deri is a 24-year-old graphic designer based in Budapest, Hungary. Besides working as a freelance designer, she is completing her Master's Degree from Moholy-Nagy University of Art and Design. She enjoys typography and a mixture of purity, class and playfulness defines her attitude towards design. Experimentation is emphasized in all of her projects. Some of her work has been published in several books and magazines.
pp.106-111

Estudio Gerundio
www.estudiogerundio.com

Gerundio, a small graphic design studio founded by Lorena Alonso in Barcelona in 2005. They focus on brand building, from corporate identity, to web design. They also work on small-scale media that include: brochures, catalogs, packaging, business cards and even wedding invitations.
pp.208-209

Face
www.designbyface.com

Face is a super modernist design studio specializing in developing honest branding projects across the world. Their work is intended to stand the test of time. Their craft is the result of constant effort, talent and commitment to quality of the highest international caliber.
Face believes the assignment contains the solution. This is why they strive to have a deep understanding of their projects and their clients' needs through their foolproof creative method – simplicity works.
pp.222-223

Farmgroup
farmgroup.co.th

Farmgroup is a Bangkok-based creative and design consultancy working across the disciplines of art and design through branding, graphic design, motion graphic, interaction, event, exhibition and installation. Their goal is to deliver innovative problem solving and design craftsmanship that is distinguished and stands the test of time.
pp.220-221

Folga
folga.ua

Folga is a creative agency providing its clients with 360° communication campaigns. Boris Zelenkevich works as art director and designer, while Andrey Zhulidin is designer and illustrator.
pp.076-077

Fundamental
fundamental-studio.com

Fundamental is a Hong Kong-based creative studio. They believe that substantial communication is the key to create and provide the best designs and solutions for their clients.
pp.128-129

Gergely Szoke
www.behance.net/nod

Gergely Szoke is a graphic designer based in Budapest, Hungary.
pp.134-137

Holt
www.holtdesign.com.au

Holt is a Sydney-based visual communications studio with an established philosophy and a fundamental belief in the role of design in communication and contemporary society. Their in-depth design knowledge, from historical to contemporary influences, theory through to practical applications, inspire design solutions that are as aesthetically arresting as they are strategically strong.
pp.068-069

Janina Dröse
www.janinadroese.de

Janina Dröse was born in Lower Saxony, Germany, in 1988. In summer 2013, she finished her Bachelor of Arts at HAWK Hildesheim, Germany. She is currently working as a freelancer. Her heart beats strongly for great branding, brilliant advertising campaigns, lovely editorial design and wonderful photographs.
pp.116-117

Jiani Lu
www.lujiani.com

Jiani Lu is a young graphic designer and photographer from Toronto, Canada. Growing up, she was inspired by visits to art galleries and museums, leading to a passion for doodling, paper cut-outs and origami at a young age. Over the years, the hands-on experience in crafts and design has translated into a key interest for print design, book binding, sewing and paper crafts.
pp.168-169

Johanna Bonnevier
www.johannabonnevier.com

Johanna Bonnevier is a Swedish art director, graphic designer and illustrator based in East London. She primarily

ranging from small and large scale print jobs to film credits and installations. Her previous and current clients include: Fashion East, b store, Embassy of Sweden, 42 architects, Lulu & Co, The Bartle School of Architecture and UCL, among others.
pp.009-011

John Wegman
www.johnwegman.com.au

John Wegman is an independent graphic designer from Melbourne, Australia. He works across various mediums with an array of clients. John is also the cofounder of Fifty North, a co-working studio for creatives.
pp.170-173

Joseph Veazey
josephveazey.com

Joseph Veazey is a designer, illustrator and artist currently working in New York City. After growing up in Atlanta and finishing school at Savannah College of Art and Design, he spent time as a designer at Adult Swim. He currently works as Art Director for NYC-based fashion designer Azede Jean-Pierre. His work has been featured in Print Magazine, American Illustration, Creative Quarterly, CMYK Magazine and various other websites and publications.
pp.070-073

Kilo
kilo.sg

Kilo is a company that combines design and technology to create experiences in the digital space.
Founded in 2005, Kilo believes that when designing for the web, art and technology are seamless and part of the creative process. Over the years, Kilo has collaborated with advertising agencies, design studios and internet startups to clearly define their digital experiences. Their areas of specialty also cover motion graphics, videos and interactive touch applications.
pp.184-185

kissmiklos
kissmiklos.com

kissmiklos is a designer and visual artist. He currently works on architecture, design and graphic design. There is an outstanding aesthetic quality and strong artistic approach that characterizes his implementation of work. His work is defined by his fine artworks, corporate identity designs and graphics.
pp.032-035, 056-059, 084-087

Kosta Rakicevic
www.kostarakicevic.com

Kosta Rakicevic was born in 1985 and currently lives and works in Belgrade, Serbia. He works in various disciplines of visual communication. Kosta founded Korak creative studio, which is focused on branding and print design.
pp.190-191

La Tortillería
latortilleria.com

Originally founded in an old tortilla factory, La Tortillería is a creative company with a passion for images and words with the exceptional ability of turning them into an exquisite reflection of an idea. They create, brand, design, publish and advertise; blending creativity and functionality to grant each project a unique personality. They are creative problem solvers who begin with the finished product in mind – either starting from scratch or from an outlined plan, they make things happen come hell or high water.
pp.080-081, 088-091

Les Bons Faiseurs
www.lesbonsfaiseurs.com

Les Bons Faiseurs is a versatile graphic design agency based in Paris. In love with great ideas and intelligent design, Les Bons Faiseurs works with a variety of brands and institutions on identities, packaging and diverse communication projects.
pp.144-145

Longton
longtondesign.com

Longton create persuasive visual concepts. Based in Melbourne, Australia, Longton provides clients around the world with design and art direction services that evoke attention and show purpose. They believe that in today's diverse media system, design must be reactive. It needs to respond to the stimulus of market demands, evoke attention and be compelling. This is precisely what drives Longton.
pp.114-115, 118-119

LSDK
lsdk.de

LSDK is a Stuttgart-based design agency, specializing in conceptual design, creation and communication. Since 2009, Christian Vögtlin and Sergej Grusdew represent their holistic principle of creation and prioritize their customers' wishes, ideas and views. Their goal is to create an emotional and informative benefit within their clients' desires that is homogeneously aligned with their corporate values.
pp.206-207

Lucas Gil-Turner
lucasgilturner.com

Lucas Gil-Turner is a full-service, multidisciplinary design and branding studio based in Madrid that specializes in creating corporate identity and branding solutions for individuals and companies. Their aim is to deliver bespoke, enduring and smart solutions with a clear and strong visual identity. They believe the strength of a good concept is in key differential factors. To reach high-quality solutions, every project is approached with rigorous methodology, creativeness and quality to detail.
They are convinced that by combining strategy and design a powerful brand, valuable asset, effective marketing tool and key differential factor are created.
pp.104-105

Luciano Marx
lucianomarx.ch

Luciano Marx is a Swiss graphic designer based in Lugano and Lausanne. His work combines and develops innovative editorial design, corporate identity, logotype, print and illustration. Luciano works with a network of artists, photographers and printers that share his philosophy.
pp.026-029

Lukasz Kulakowski
emptypage.pl

Lukasz Kulakowski is a brand and type designer, illustrator and creative art director currently based in Ireland. He also runs a small brand studio – emptypage. His works have been featured in Smashing Magazine, Gallery, Los Logos and on Adobe Max Keynote 2013. His works consist of minimalistic, clean and geometric style, good lettering and typography with custom illustration.
pp.210-211

Manic Design
www.wearemanic.com

Manic Design is an award-winning creative agency with a portfolio of work that ranges from websites and online campaigns, to advertising and branding.
The studio was founded in 1999 with the belief that good design always includes both creativity and communication. A piece of work that looks great, but fails to speak to its audience, is not good design. The team have embraced this and cemented it into their culture and their work.
pp.094-095

Mash Creative
www.mashcreative.co.uk

Mash Creative is an independent design studio based in East London and Essex. They work on creative projects that include identity and branding, print media and web design. In a short space of time they have acquired a reputation for producing innovative and effective graphic design that is engaging, clear and relevant. They don't believe in just one approach, which is why their work is always unique – producing relevant and successful solutions that add value to their clients' brands.
pp.122-123

moodley brand identity
www.moodley.at

moodley brand identity is an owner-led, award-winning strategic design agency with offices in Vienna and Graz. Since 1999, moodley has worked together with its customers to develop corporate and product brands that live, breathe and grow. moodley believes that the key contribution is to analyze complex requirements and develop simple, smart solutions with emotional appeal – whether they are corporate start-up, product launch or brand positioning. The team currently consists of more than 40 employees.
pp.092-093, 180-181

Mother Design

motherdesign.com

Mother Design is a design and branding group within the advertising agency, Mother New York. They create fully integrated brand communications that are anchored in strategy, culture and design. During their seven years experience, they've made identity systems, books, billboards, apps, films, websites, packages, whiskey, political t-shirts, environments and more.
pp.150-153, 230-232

MYDE

www.mydestudio.com

MYDE studio was founded in Syktyvkar in 2009. They specialize in design and support of visual communications in both real and virtual environments for corporate and product brands, which are either active in the market, strating up or need rebranding. MYDE are equally interested in working with both small companies and large businesses from a variety of sectors.
They work with clients who value creative and practical ideas and the importance of design to create a strong brand. Design is a sales tool that increases the value of a brand, making it stand out from the competition and become a leader in its category, or, increase customer loyalty. They analyze client needs, assess the situation on the market, identify the strengths of the company and develop a clear, efficient, functional and attractive high-quality communication solution, taking into account the needs of the client and the target audience.
pp.218

Nueve estudio

www.n-u-e-v-e.com

Nueve is a design and consulting studio co-founded by Ana V. Francés and Cristina Toledo in Valencia, Spain. Their work has received numerous awards, both at home and abroad. Their projects have been featured in many exhibitions, books and trade publications and they are proud members of the Valencian Community Designers Association (ADCV).
pp.146-147

Olssøn Barbieri

olssonbarbieri.com

Olsson Barbieri is a design agency specializing in brand identity and packaging design with particular focus on wine and spirits, luxury goods, fashion, culture and art industries. Founded with the intention of working independently and without compromising conceptual development and quality of execution, the company evolves by pursuing new standards of design through research and experimentation. Henrik Olsson and Erika Barbieri founded Olsson Barbieri in 2005. Since then they have been published and awarded by national and international juries.
pp.162

Onion Design

www.oniondesign.com.tw

Onion Design is a multi-disciplinary graphic design studio whose work covers brand identity and development, art direction, advertising, motion and printed literature. They believe that design should stem from good ideas, no matter how big or small they are. The team strives to create work

that excites, inspires and most importantly, meets the needs of clients.
pp.212-215

Paperlux

www.paperlux.com

Nestled in a timber framework house in the very happening Schanzenviertel neighborhood in Hamburg, Paperlux is driven by devotion when it comes to design and concepts for, on, in, and with paper. Pioneers in their own right, the staff of 11 greet the medium of paper with inspiration, artistry, and passion, which they implement to create design and communication concepts of excellence.
pp.174-175

Paprika

www.paprika.com

Paprika is a graphic design and strategic marketing firm specializing in business communications services, corporate identity programs, branding, annual reports, brochures, catalogues, posters, packaging, environmental design, signs and websites. Since opening its doors for business in 1991, Paprika has won more than 700 national and international awards for design excellence including: Aiga, Applied Arts annual awards, Art Directors Club and Type Directors Club of New York, British Design and Art Direction, among many others.
pp.154-159, 188-189

Pentagram

www.pentagram.com

Pentagram is the world's largest independent design consultancy. The firm was founded in 1972 and is run by sixteen partners – a group of friends who are all leaders in their individual creative fields. Working from offices in London, New York, Austin and Berlin, the firm specializes in different areas of graphic design and industrial design and architecture, producing printed materials, environments, products and interactive media for a wide range of international clients.
pp.176-179

Porcelain Studio

www.porcelainstudio.net

At Porcelain Studio, the team observes the world from an imaginative perspective, making each project special and unique.
For them, a good project is one that starts with a strong conceptual basis, develops an attractive graph and exudes contemporary design.
pp.112-113

Raum Mannheim

raum-mannheim.com

Raum Mannheim conceptualizes and creates the visual presence for their clients and places them on the scene with graphics, texts, illustrations, installations and photography. The team loves the challenge of understanding complex subjects, of giving them structure and precisely implementing them through different media forms. They think holistically; for them, quality lies in detail.
It is not the size of the project, but rather the project-specific tasks and the individual forms it takes on – starting

from an unusual idea, working to a coherent concept and seeing it through to a unique aesthetic expression.
Through their own artwork, projects and exhibitions, they are constantly expanding their creative spectrum.
pp.200-203, 226-227

saad branding+design

saad-studio.com

saad is a branding and design studio. They build brands that talk to people and create relationships — not in an ordinary way, but rather, in a way that makes them unique and exclusive. Thereby, the studio adds the strategic nature of branding and its expertise in design and creates brands that become unique and truly relevant.
pp.012-013

Sasha Astron

www.behance.net/astron

Sasha Astron is a multidisciplinary designer based in Kiev, Ukraine. He has compiled a vast portfolio in graphic design, web design, branding, 3D graphics, advertising, illustration and art direction.
pp.024-025

Simon Laliberté

www.behance.net/slaliberte

Simon Laliberté is a graphic designer and art director. He graduated from the University of Quebec at Montréal in 2012 and remains based in Montréal. He specializes in branding, packaging, screen-printing and the development of new ideas and projects.
pp.182-183

Simon McWhinnie

www.smc-design.co.uk

Simon McWhinnie is a 26-year-old Norwich-based graphic designer with a passion for branding and creative problem solving across a variety of disciplines. He lives by the 'smile in the mind' theory and enjoys work that involves a witty, memorable and conceptual based approach to design.
pp.020-021

Smörgåsbord

smorgasbordstudio.com

Smörgåsbord is an independent branding and graphic design studio based in Cardiff and Amsterdam, offering "Branding, Strategy and Art Direction – a selection of good things."
They adopt a scaleable approach – assembling bespoke teams of talented international individuals for each project, allowing them to work across a wide range of inspiring projects of various sizes.
Their strategic capability, coupled with rigorous art direction, result in strong brand narratives and memorable, engaging design. They believe in the strength and purity of an idea and their aim is to deliver creative excellence.
pp.055, 130-131

Snask

snask.com

Snask is an internationally renowned design, brand and film company that create the heart and soul of brands. They

create new brands and rejuvenate old ones. They knock out branded material for print, web, film and experimental advertising. Their name means candy, filth and gossip and everywhere they travel they make a couple of enemies, but a million more fans. Snask off!
pp. 030-031

Solene Leblanc
www.soleneleblanc.com

Solene Leblanc is a French designer, living and working in London. After studying for three years in Brussels, she earned a Master of Arts and graduated with distinction in Graphic Design from the London College of Communication. Since then, she has been developing effective, well-crafted design solutions for a wide range of clients, while continuing to work on self-initiated projects. Approaching every project from a cross media perspective, she has a strong interest in typography and swears by simplicity.
pp.142-143

Spaincreative
www.spaincreative.es

Spaincreative came about in the best possible way a design, publicity and communication agency can – from experience. Spaincreative's strength is in its way of thinking, that's what makes it different from the rest. Don't wait for a miracle to happen – act, create and solve. They adapt themselves to any terrain whether it is uphill, downhill or flat – they are creative in any environment!
p.216-217

StudioMakgill
www.studiomakgill.com

StudioMakgill is a Brighton-based design studio founded in 2007 by Hamish Makgill. They create simple, beautiful, intuitive design that allows their clients to connect with their audience.
The team focuses on the creation of brand identities that work as well in print as they do on screen. They work for a range of clients within a variety of sectors and they're as comfortable creating an identity for a range of cosmetics, as they are a look and feel for a successful tapas restaurant in north London.
They're passionate about good design and revel in the detail of a project. They look to inspire their clients whilst having a lasting effect on their business.
pp.124-127

TGIF
www.tgif.com.hk

TGIF is a Hong Kong-based graphic design and branding studio that was established in 2010.
They provide a full range of design services including branding, corporate communications, web design, marketing materials, packaging, exhibition and event design. TGIF believes that their creative thinking brings out positive energy and provoking solutions to their clients.
pp.040-043

The Forgery
www.theforgery.se

The Forgery is a creative agency based in Sweden. They cover brand platforms, logo design, web development and high-end print. They specialize in mobile optimized websites, so called responsive design, but happily work in a variety of media and platforms.
pp.224-225

The Rainy Monday
www.therainymonday.com

Xavier Martinez and Iñaki Cabréra casually decided to start doing work together. They called their collaboration, The Rainy Monday, creating amazing stories, rain or shine. Today, they are a flourishing advertising agency where Martinez is Creative Director and Cabrera, Copy Writer.
pp.074-075

We Made This
www.wemadethis.co.uk

We Made This is a graphic design studio based in London specializing in delectable print work. Alistair Hall founded the studio in 2004 and its clients include Penguin Books, the National Trust, the Crafts Council, Tricycle Theatre, Historic Royal Palaces and ITV.
pp.228-229

Winnie Wu
www.studiokaleido.net

Winnie Wu is a contemporary designer and graphic artist based in Singapore and Shanghai.
Creative Director of progressive agency studio KALEIDO, she wears multiple hats as designer, illustrator and curator. Best known for her street-wise designs, she has been featured in numerous publications such as Asia-Pacific Design and New Generation in Asia Creative. Her work has been exhibited or commissioned by Kult, Tiger Translate, Nixon, Canon, 42below and Zouk.
pp.132-133

Yerevan Dilanchian
www.yerevan-dilanchian.com

Yerevan Dilanchian is a Sydney based designer and illustrator. He previously completed a Bachelor's in Design at the College of Fine Arts, University of New South Wales, specializing in graphic design and applied object design. Dilanchian's works are primarily print focused, allowing him to explore tactile and bespoke creative solutions. His aesthetic is primarily geometric and clean-cut.
pp.018-019, 078-079

Acknowledgements

We would like to acknowledge our gratitude to the artists and designers for their generous contributions of images, ideas and concepts. We are very grateful to many other people whose names do not appear on the credits but who provided assitance and support. Thanks also go to people who have worked hard on the book and put ungrudging efforts into it. Without you all, the creation and ongoing development of this book would not have been possible and thank you for sharing your innovation and creativity with all our readers.